Published by
ATLANTIC®
PUBLISHERS & DISTRIBUTORS
B-2, Vishal Enclave, Opp. Rajouri Garden,
New Delhi-110027
Phones : 25413460, 25429987, 25466842

Sales Office
7/22, Ansari Road, Darya Ganj,
New Delhi-110002
Phones : 23273880, 23275880, 23280451
Fax : 91-11-23285873
web : www.atlanticbooks.com
e-mail : info@atlanticbooks.com

ISBN 81-269-0482-8

Printed in India
at Nice Printing Press, Delhi

PREFACE

I feel great pleasure to place in the hands of the readers my 27th book on Library and Information Science. Classified catalogue is not a new concept as Dr. Ranganathan—a renowned personality in the field of library science—had specialised in it long before in 1924-25 from University College, London. Not fully convinced with the European mind of Dictionary Catalogue, Dr. Ranganathan evolved a new system that brought about a revolution in the field of cataloguing. His *Classified Catalogue Code* received tremendous success and is held the most ideal and the greatest contribution to the subject. His book highlights the practical aspects of classified catalogue as per classified code.

Dr. Ranganathan's book has been referred to by almost all authors in this field. My present book *A Practice—Handbook of Classified Catalogue* too has been written on the same concept. It is a fresh addition to the available collection of books on the subject. I have made utmost efforts to provide a comparatively more detailed study and an easy understanding of the practical cataloguing. The book has been structured into three parts: Part I nicely introduces the readers to the concepts of Classified Catalogue, Typography, Document and Pagination; Part II is a complete treatise on the Entry aspect of cataloguing; and Part III richly provides Practical Examples so as to enable the readers to have a comfortable, genuine and firm grasp of the subject. The language of the book has been deliberately kept simple so that it is easily accessible to the average readers.

It is hoped that the book would be an asset for those interested in library science. It will be highly useful to the teachers and students and the practising librarians who are engaged in learning and working in cataloguing field.

In writing this book, I have been fortunate to have had help and inspiration from my daughter Dr Alka Rawat who not only encouraged me to write this book and serve the library profession but also supported me in all my professional and academic endeavours.

I am thankful to M/s Atlantic Publishers and Distributors, New Delhi, for publishing my book in a short time span.

C.K. SHARMA

CONTENTS

PART – I

INTRODUCTORY PART

1

CLASSIFIED CATALOGUE

(Based on Classified Catalogue Code (1964) & Cataloguing Practice (Ed 2:1975) of Dr. S.R. Ranganathan)

Introduction

Dr. Ranganathan inspired to learn about Cataloguing. A sense of revolt induced in his mind while learning Cataloguing in 1924-25 in the school of librarianship in the University College, College of London. During the learning Dr. Ranganathan learned teaching techniques of Cataloguing. He studied Anglo-American Code (A3) of 1908 without any if and but he was so clear in his mind about the structure, complexity of author entry, subject entries and the drawback that he thought of create new thought and system which can create a revolution in the field of Cataloguing. Dr. Ranganathan was not convinced with the European mind of dictionary Catalogue. He was of the view that reader's first approach is subject. Other approaches come afterward.

There were mainly two libraries in Great Britain where Classified Catalogue was in practice. One was Central Library of Pittsburgh and other was Mitchel Library of Glasgow. It was all in practice. But there was no theory based on rules. Dr. Ranganathan learned nothing about Classified Catalogue in class. Only rules which were taught were for Dictionary Catalogue of A.A. Code. He also experienced that the teachers of the school of librarianship at London emphasise more on format, collation, imprint in its practical class. There were many signs and symbols used in format of main entry. However Dr. Ranganathan discussed many problems and also convinced with Classified system of Cataloguing. But he wanted some times more clear rational and modified.

When Dr. Ranganathan returned to Madras he was given free hand to work in the library and run the library according to his own system and practices. He reorganized the Madras University Library and allowed open access the simplified library working. So far Cataloguing and Classification is concerned he started reference service. He made selection of qualified staff who could maintain public relations. All these steps could resulted to miracle change in library functioning *i.e.*

(a) There was an access increased from 500 to 6000 volume a year; the Cataloguing already applied in Madras university was based on British Museum code and moreover it was modified arbitrarily here and there.

(b) Dr. Ranganathan studied the nature of readers, their interest and reading habits.

(c) Dr. Ranganathan selected two colleagues C. Sundaram and K.M. Sivaraman to assist in his work. They were free from library working traditions. They were fresh graduates and hard working and industrious.

(d) It was the routine of three—Dr. Ranganathan, Sundaram and Sivraman—to discuss various problems once a week in the light of experienced gained.

(e) Dr. Ranganathan established a School of Library Science in 1929 and started teaching Cataloguing to the students.

The First step

During his starting service and revolutionary steps during 1926-1932 Dr. Ranganathan Classified 7000 Volumes and also Catalogued. During 1931-32 Dr. Ranganathan started writing and practicing Colon Classification but at conscious level. Though Classified Catalogue Code was not shaped, he continued teaching Cataloguing till 1933. Colon Classification was published in the year of 1933.

Journey-intuition

After the publication of Colon Classification, Dr. Ranganathan had to go to Calcutta and it was a journey of 38 hours. He took plenty of slips of 5" × 3" and few sharpened pencils. It was a peaceful atmosphere in the journey. Moreover, beautiful scenes and a fresh air which could concentrate Dr. Ranganathan to think and work seriously on cataloguing. He memorized many problems and thought of their solution based on his experiences made with various readers in his library. He practiced various problems and experienced the difficulties. He formulated various rules of Classified Catalogue Code. On his return from Calcutta he discussed the problem with his colleagues and again checked up them and practiced them in library. He prepared the press copy and got it typed. It was first formulation of Classified Catalogue Code. It was a draft copy which was prepared and typed for further action.

Dr. Ranganathan was a man of noble thoughts and dedicated personality. The press copy was on his table and he was in between the two minds whether to publish it or recheck it. He was perhaps likely to request the vice-chancellor of Madras University for its printing. Suddenly Mr. Natasa Anand a spiritual friend of Dr. Ranganathan came with a copy of A.A. Code for comments. However, by the time W.B. Yeast of Ireland send a copy along with the letter from Rudolph Gujielsngs, chairman and Editor-in-Chief of Cataloguing revision committee of ALA, in which there were suggestions and also different views on the terminology of Dr. Ranganathan. However, Dr. Ranganathan discussed the matter of the letter, made few correction but did not agree on terminology and terms. Ranganathan again compared these canons applying in A.A. Code and C.C.C. He finalized the study and result was the publication of *Theory of Library Cataloguing*. The other effort was the publication of another book *Headings and Canons* in 1938.

During the lifetime of Dr. Ranganathan the *Classified Catalogue Code* he revised five times with many additions, modifications and deletions.

Edition First. It was publication service of Madras Library Association. The important point of this publication was that it was distributed among the libraries and the librarians to reach to concrete form and to do their day-to-day work of Cataloguing to make full use of all the entries in the Card Catalogue and also provisions reference service to readers. Mr. Sayer pronounced this work "by far and largest contribution to the subject".

Edition Second. It was published in 1945 which incorporated —

Canons enunciated in 1938.

Theory of alphabetization (in Theory of Lib Cataloguing) This theory separated 'Legislative Phase and Executive Phase' in Alphabetization.

Edition Third. It came out in 1951 with addition of —

Rules for a Union Catalogue of periodical publication.

Rules for abstraction periodicals.

Rules for Sanskrit Sutras.

Edition Fourth. It came out in 1955 with addition of —

Supplementary rules of National bibliography.

Rule for style of writing.

Separate problem of determine the author and choice of headings.

Changes in rules of alphabetization.

Edition Fifth. It came out in 1964 with additions of following rules along with rules of Dictionary Catalogue —

Chapter CD – Law of Symmetry

Chapter DD – Physical form

Chapter DE – Centralized Cataloguing

Chapter KK – Homonym in Class Index headings

Chapter KL – Feature headings

Part V – Non-conventional documents

Publication of Cataloguing. The last book which Dr. Ranganathan wrote was Cataloguing Practice in 1950 and it also revised but published in 1975 after his death. This book is for practical cataloguing. This does not contains the rules but reduced the rules. Dr. Ranganathan made some modification in code but CCC could not revised accordingly due to his sudden death in 1972. However these modification have been added in this book "Cataloguing Practice".

RULES FOR CLASSIFIED CATALOGUE

Equipment for Practical Work in Cataloguing

A Cataloguer or the student of Cataloguing should equip himself with the following —

A copy of CCC

Catalogue slips or cards of 5" × 3"

A pen with the sharp nib

A hard pencil

One card Catalogue cabinet drawer

Shelf list card 5" × 2"

Cutters list

Endless Spiral of Development in Cataloguing

1. New type of reading material
2. Proper interpretation of rules
3. Necessary amendments and interpretation of rules
4. Following of Normative principles
5. Difficult kind of library service in practice
6. New normative principles should replace the old ones on the basis of experiences and observations
7. Implication of five law of library science
8. Application of canons of cataloguing

Canons of Cataloguing

These are Normative principles applicable to cataloguing for —

(a) Drafting of a catalogue code and formulation of rules

(b) Interpretation of rules to meet new situations

(c) Provision of suitable guidance for Cataloguing work

Terms in Reference

1. **Law.** Major discipline *i.e.* library science.

2. **Canon.** First order of major discipline *i.e.* Book selection, Classification, Cataloguing.

3. **Principle.** Later order of major discipline *i.e.* Facet sequence in Classification and Alphabetization in Cataloguing.

There are nine Canons of Cataloguing

1. Canon of Ascertainability
2. Canon of Prepotence
3. Canon of Individualization

4. Canon of Sought-headings
5. Canon of Context
6. Canon of Permanence
7. Canon of Currency
8. Canon of Consistence
9. Canon of Recall Value

Principles of Cataloguing

1. Laws of Interpretations. A Catalogue code is like a legal document. Any rules in it should be interpreted like a legal text. There may be a conflict between one rule and another. This law helps in resolving the conflict with the aid of law of interpretation.

2. Law of Impartiality. This principle helps in use of heading on preferential basis, on sufficient grounds and not arbitrarily.

Example :

In case of Joint authorship

In case of Multiple services

In case of Locus statement

3. Law of Symmetry. If there are two entities, or situations which are counterpart of each other. If one of the entities of the situations is given weight in any particular context, the other entity or situation should also be given a corresponding weight.

4. Law of Parsimony. If there are two or more possible alternative rules hearing on a particular phenomenon, the one is to be preferred which leads to overall economy of man power, material, money and time together with proper weight age.

Example :

Chain procedure

Printed or written card

5. Principle of Local Variation. This Principal guide in case of problems of local variations regarding —

(a) Local Catalogue code at national and regional level

(b) Linguistic Catalogue code

(c) Local code of each individual library
(d) Consistency without any mutual contradiction
(e) Lower link supplemented to all the upper links

Example :

Punctuation system of artificial language
Style of writing and printing
Arrangement of entries
Rendering of Personal names
Entry element
Script and transliteration
Analytical entries

6. Principle of osmosis. If there is change in the Catalogue Code or in the scheme of classification on the basis of canon of context.

Function of the Catalogue

A library is essentially a tool. Library Catalogue should be so designed as to —

1. Disclose to every reader his or her document;
2. Secure for every document its reader;
3. Save the time of the reader; and for this purpose
4. Save the time of the staff.

Function of Catalogue on Cutters Line of Approach

1. Enable a person how to find a book of which either the
   - A Author, or
   - B Title, or
   - C Subject is known;
2. Show what the library has
   - D by a given author,
   - E on a given subject, and
   - F in a given kind of literature; and
3. Assist in the choice of a book as to its
   - G Edition
   - H Character

Physical form of the Library Catalogue

1. **Book form.** It may be printed or manuscript. Nearly a century ago Jewett wrote an epigraph of the printed Catalogue while addressing a conference of librarians held in New York City.

2. **Card form.** It is in common use in libraries. But it is not the last physical form.

3. **Micro-film form.**

Language of Entries

1. **Favoured language.** It means the language of the library. In other words the language in which the majority of the document of the library occur.

2. **Many language document.** Favoured languages should be given first place and other languages should be given second or so in descending scale of popularity.

3. **Non-favoured language**

(a) Proper name should be entered in the language in which it occurs.

(b) The title of a document is to be written in the language in which it occurs on the title page.

(c) If title page is given in two or more languages it is to be written in most popular language.

(d) If the title of the document is not in favoured language and it is not a proper noun, but is descriptive, its translation in the favoured language may be added within square brackets as a separate sentence in title section, either in the main entry along or also in specific added entry.

Script of the Entries

It must be —

(a) Script of favoured language, or

(b) Any other script chosen for the library,

(c) Favoured script,

(d) If the title page is not in favoured scripts of the library the word taken from the title page are to be transliterated in that script.

ARTICLES AND CONTRACTIONS

Articles

Arabic: ad, al, ar, as, at, ez

Dutch: de, het, 't , een, eene

French: le, la, bs, un, une

English: a, an, the

Hebrew: ba, be

Hungaria: a, az, egy

Italian: gli, gl, i, il, l, la, le, lo, un

Spanish: el, la, lo, los, un, una

Portuguese: a, as, o, un, una

Contractions

Abridged	-	Abr
Annotated	-	Annot
Annotation	-	Annot
Author	-	Auth
Before Christ	-	BC
Commentary	-	Comm
Century	-	Cent
Complied	-	Comp
Dedication	-	Ded
Director	-	Dir
Edited	-	Ed
Editors	-	Ed
Edition	-	Ed
Epitomized	-	Epit
Fascicle	-	Fasc
Heft	-	H
Illustration	-	Ill
Illustrator	-	Ill
Introduction	-	Introd
Number	-	N
Overset	-	Overs
Pages	-	P

Popular	-	Pop
Preface	-	Pref
Pseudonym	-	Pseud
Report	-	Rep
Reporter	-	Rep
Revised	-	Rev
Reviser	-	Rev
Special	-	Sp
Translated	-	Tr
Translators	-	Tr
Translations	-	Tr
Vertaler	-	Vert
Volume (s)	-	V

Style of Writing

1. Size of catalogue card

(a) 124 × 75 × 0.25mm

12.5 × 7.5cm

5" × 3"

2. Writing flued. The Indelibility of ink used should be such as to make the entry last as long as the Card lasts. Card is supposed to be permanent record.

3. Use of pencil. Call number and Class number should however be in pencil. Because these are liable to revision and change.

4. Library hand. All words and number in an entry are to be in a bold upright hand, their letter and digits being detached from one another.

Roman script

A B C D E F G H I J K L M N O P Q R S T U V W X Y Z

a b c d e f g h i j k l m n o p q r s t u v w x y z

Indo-Arabic Numerals

1 2 3 4 5 6 7 8 9 0

5. Lines in an entry

(a) Leading line – The topmost horizontal line of card.

(b) First vertical – The left most vertical line of a card.

(c) Second vertical – The vertical line which is to the right of the first vertical of a card.

6. Leading section. It is a section beginning on the leading line — and all its continuation lines are to be commenced at the first vertical.

7. Sections starting from Second vertical. All sections except Index number sections, Accession number section, the section in a Series Index entry.

Continuation lines from first vertical.

8. Index Number Section. It is to be as far to the right as possible. In the section preceding it or in the first line after the said last line.

Index Number Section

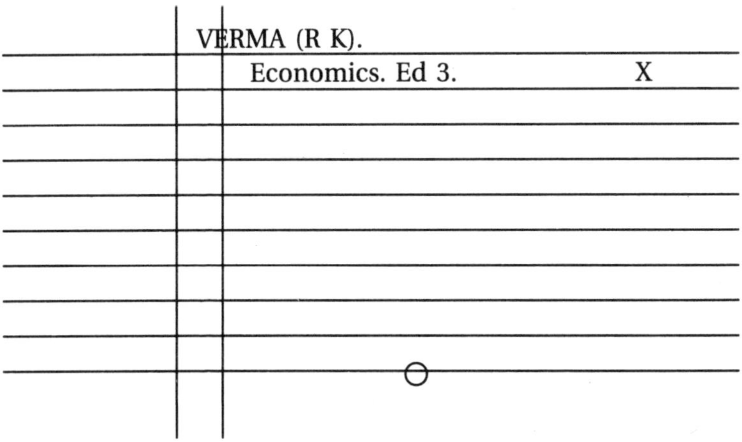

9. Serial Number in Series Book Index Entry. The serial number in the second section of a series Index Entry is to be commenced at the second vertical or as far further its right as may be necessary if the serial number is so long as to go beyond the second vertical.

10. Accession Number Section. The accession number section is to begin at the first vertical of the bottom most line.

2:55 N9
SHARMA (C K).
Handbook of colon classification.
Ed. 2.

3245

Accession Number Section

11. Two or more Accession Number. If there are two more Accession Number to be written in the same main Entry, they are to be recorded in a sequence parallel to that of the Book Number to which they correspond.

2:55 N9
SHARMA (C K).
Handbook of colon classification. Ed 2.

548-56

2

TYPOGRAPHY

1. Entry Element. The words other than auxiliary words, is an entry element in a block in a heading are to be in Block Letters.

2. A Directing element is to be underlined. In print it is to be in italics.

3. Descriptive Element. A Description element is to be underlined. In print it is to be in italics. The first letter of each word in it other than an auxiliary word is to be in Capital.

4. Numerals. All numbers are to be written in Indo-Arabic numerals, except —

(a) Those forming part of the name of the monarch of Pape.

(b) Those forming part of the name of other person or of a corporate body.

(c) Those usually written in Roman Numerical.

(d) Those of call numbers and Class Numbers.

5. Punctuation Marks

(a) A comma is to separate two consecutive Blocks in a heading.

(b) A comma is to separate a Description element in a Block in a heading from what it describes.

(c) Circular brackets are to enclose each individualising and Secondary Elements.

(d) The conjunction between by a comma. If this is done Semicolon should precede a Description element instead of comma.

VARIETIES OF NOTATIONS

1. Inclusive Notations

Example : 3 – 18

2. Years. If the number denote years, the Second member of the inclusive notation is to consist of —

(a) The last digit alone when earlier digits are common to both the members;

(b) The last two digits alone when earlier digits are common to both the members; and

(c) So on.

Example : 1962 – 3
1952 – 63
1963 – 2221

3. Open Notation

Example : 3 –

4. Non-Consecutive

Examples : 3 – 18
41 – 57
85 –

SIZE OF BOOKS

Each library maintains the Volumes of following specifications —

1. Undersized; or
2. Oversized; or
3. Abnormal (having too many plates or maps)

Undersized. In breadth is less than 300mm, and thickness is not minimum than 5mm or thickness is not greater than 30mm and its height is less than 150mm or thickness is not greater than 50mm and its height is less than 120mm or thickness is not greater than 150mm and its height is less than 50mm.

Oversized. Breadth is not less than 300mm.

Abnormal Size

(a) It contains not less than 50 plates or maps or both plates and maps taken together.

(b) Paper is very poor or impressed paper or paper loaded with clay.

Treatment of different size of document in Book Number

(a) Undersized volume is underlined – N3

(b) Oversized volume is overlined – M14

(c) Abnormal volume is underlined and K15 overlined

If Main Entry or added entries are split-over to next card [Rule E F]

If an entry is too long for one card and it is to be continued in another card, the following phrases will be recorded on the cards.

MAIN ENTRY — FIRST CARD

1. The connecting phrases 'Continued in the next card' is to be at the right end of the bottom-most line of the earlier card and the connecting word 'Continued' is to be at the right end of the top of the latter card.

```
2:55N3 QN64;N88
        RANGANATHAN (S R) (1965-72).
        Classified Catalogue Code: with
additional rules for Dictionary
Catalogue code. Ed.5. Assisted by
A Neelmeghan (1927).
        (Ranganathan series in
library science 2).

                    Continued in the next card
```

MAIN ENTRY SECOND CARD

		Continued
	2:55N3 QN64;N88	
		Bibliography : p. 608-9
	531	

2. A sequence of Main entry of periodical publications, having the same class number in their respective leading sections, written in different cards because of—
   (a) break in the set, or
   (b) change of name, or
   (c) any other causes

   should be treated as a set of 'continued cards'
3. If the set of 'continued cards' consist of three or more cards —

FIRST CARD

		Continued in the next card 2

(a) The first card is to have the connecting phase at the bottom only; the last card is to have the connecting phrase (word) at the top only.

(b) The intermediate cards are to have connecting phrase (word) at the top as well as at the bottom.

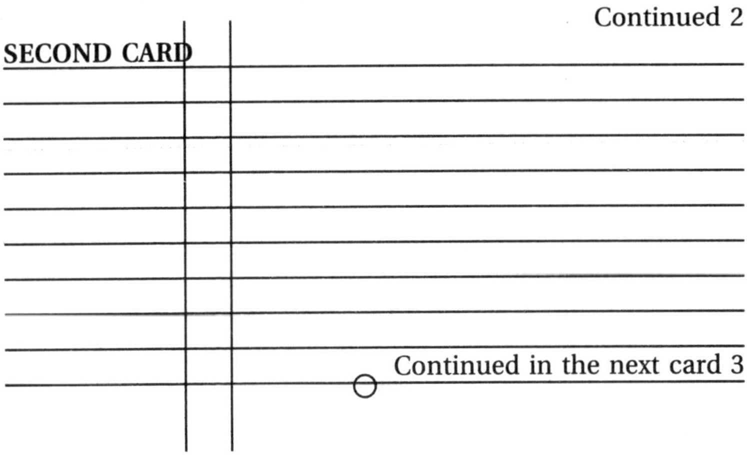

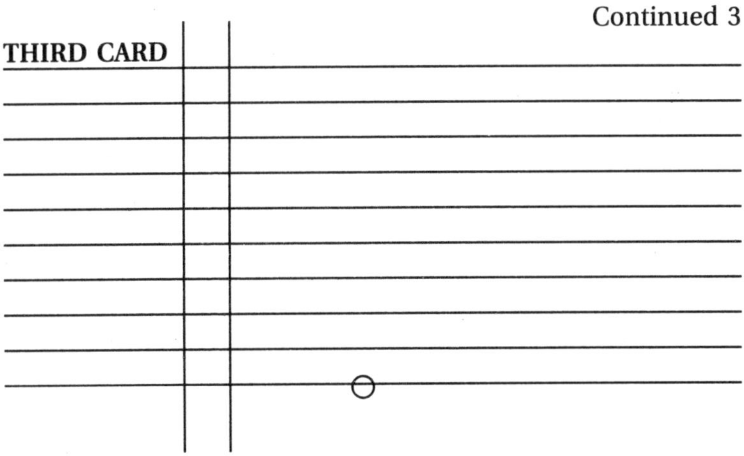

4. The 'continued cards' are to be numbered serially, the serial number being written after the connecting word 'continued' near the top of the card.

3

Document

[Rule FE]

Document is a Embodied thought and a record of work on paper or other material fit for physical handlings, transport across space and preservation through time.

1. Macro Document. Usually a work expressing macro thought is embodied in to a document all by itself. Such a document may be called Macro-Document.

Example : Books

2. Micro-Document. Usually a work expressing micro thought is not embodied in to a document all by itself. Several Micro Documents are embodied in one and the same document. In this way several Micro-Documents are Clubbed together in a single Macro-Document embodied in it.

Example : Periodical is Macro-document but each article in it is Micro-document.

Example : Periodical – Annals of library science (Host Document or Locus)

Articles : Indian National Bibliography (Micro-document)

KINDS OF DOCUMENTS

I. 1. Conventional documents

(a) Printed book

(b) Periodical publication

Example : International library progress

(c) Serial

Example : Statesman's year book

2. Indexing periodical example — Law Index

(a) Abstracting periodical.

Example : Biological abstract

(b) Reviewing periodical.

Example : Annual review of Bio-chemistry

3. Books

(a) Single book

(b) Multi volume book

4. Composite book

(a) Ordinary composite book

(b) Artificial composite book

5. Incunabula

A book printed within a few decades of the invention of modern printing – *i.e.* in 15th Century.

II. Non-Conventional Documents

1. Reprographs

(a) Photographic

(b) Sound record

(c) Speaking book

(d) Camera reels

(e) Visual documents

(f) Audio-Visual document.

4

Pagination

(Different pages) [Rule FG]

Pages are recorded in many sections and in different position. They are ascertained in title page overflow pages and also from other sources other than the document.

Pagination takes its place in —

1. Imprint
2. Physical description
3. Bibliography
4. Note Section
5. Analytical entries

Kinds of Pages

1. Preliminary pages – i, ii, iii.......ix........Lxi
2. Main pages – 1, 2, 3, 4, 5......100.........500
3. Last series of pages of the end of documents
4. Integral pages – 11, 111, 12, 121, 122...........15, 151........7, 711
5. Bibliography pages —

   These pages are sometimes given in different type or sometimes pick out of the main pages.

   Example : Book has 350 pages but last 10 pages belongs to bibliography 340

   = Main pages 340

   Bibliography pages 341 – 50

   i.e. 340 + 10 = 350 pages

Various types of Catalogue

There are many kinds of catalogue:

1. **Library Catalogue.** The list of document in a library and in a collection forming a portion of it.

2. **Union Catalogue.** Catalogue of two more libraries where copies of each document can be found. It may cover all kinds of documents or any restricted kind of them.

3. **Documentation list.** It is a list of documents listed together for some purpose. It is also a selected list of documents relevant to the pursuit of his enquiry or study.

4. **Bibliography.** It is commonly known as list of Macro-documents.

5. **Micro-Bibliography.** It is a bibliography exclusively or mostly of Micro-documents.

6. **National Bibliography.** It is a list of books and periodicals published in a country or published by a countryman.

7. **Linguistic Bibliography.** It is a list of the books and periodicals published in a language.

PART – II

ENTRY PART

5

Entry

Entry is a ultimate unit record in a Catalogue or a documentation list.

MAIN ENTRY

It is a specific entry giving maximum information about whole of a document.

All other entries — specific or general — relating to the document, are normally derived from main entry.

I. Source of Information

(a) Main source of information for preparing main entry is Title page. The main entry is to be made up of a reproduction of a portion of a title page modified according to prescribed rules, utilising if necessary, any relevant information given in the overflow of the title page.

(b) If the title page had not been printed or it is defaced or removed and could not be copied from any other book, the title page may be reconstructed from any source.

(c) If there are two or more title pages, the one may be chosen for cataloguing purpose which is special to the document catalogue and generic title page common to several documents or which is the language of the library or in favoured language.

(d) If the title page is polyglot, the portion to be chosen for cataloguing purposes.

Main Entry Sections

The main Entry is to consist successively of following sections :

Sequence

1. Leading Section
2. Heading Section
3. Title Section
4. Note Section
5. Accession Number Section
6. Tracing Section

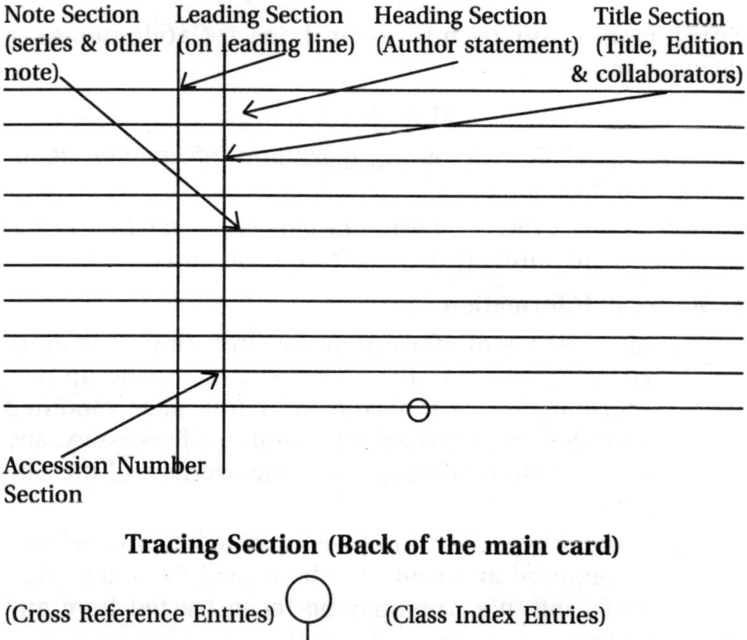

Tracing Section (Back of the main card)

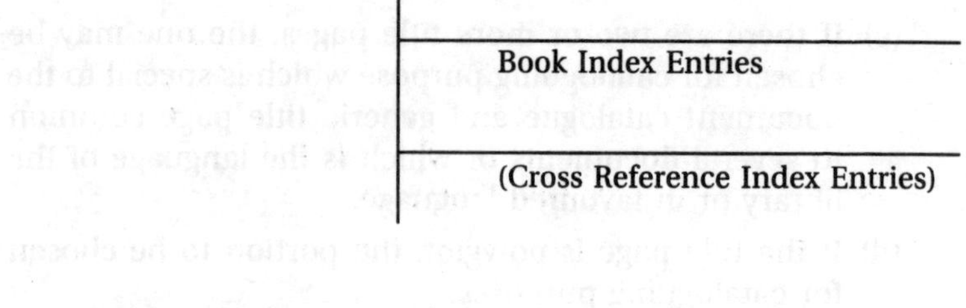

Information not to include in the Main Entry (Rule MBI–G)

1. As it is not a inventory Catalogue hence all details cannot be given in Main Entry. Only selected and useful information are given in Main Entry.

2. Imprint. This Section is omitted in CCC and hence no mention in main Entry (Place of publisher, Name of publisher, Year of publication). This is a age of open access system and library service, which is rightly compared to workshop rather than a museum as Imprinted is seldom sought by the majority of readers and therefore regarded unnecessary as it overcrowd the card. Such information are also given in Trade Bibliographies or the Accession Register.

3. Collation. Collation (pages, material, size) is also omitted in Main Entry. These informations are not commonly demanded by the reader as these informations are readily available in bibliographies and the Accession Register. Therefore it is regarded as unnecessary overcrowding the card.

Information given less importance in Main Entry

There are few information and the section, which are given less weightage in comparison to other information mentioned in Main Entry *i.e.* Accession Number and Tracing Section.

1. Accession Number. It is given less weightage and hence it is not intended for the reader's eye. Its to be written at the left end of the bottom most line of the card to the minimum. It is to act as a link between the Accession Register and the Catalogue.

2. Tracing Section. The purpose of tracing section is to facilitate the removal of the related cards when a book is weeded out from the library. It also help in coordinating the work of the technical section of the time of Cataloguing.

Number of Main Entry

There is one and only one main entry for each document. It enters its Chief specific subject. It is a basic entry for the document. All other entries are derived from it. It gives us more information about document than any other entry.

(A) Leading Section. The Leading Section is to consist of the Call Number of the document :

1. Class Number
2. Two Spaces
3. Book Number
4. Two spaces
5. Collection Number — It is rarely found. If any it may also be written above the book number.

Style of Writing

1. It is written by pencil.
2. It is written in library hand.
3. It starts from first vertical.
4. No full stop is put after Call Number.

Basis

It is based on Classification Scheme. The Call Number would have been assigned by the Classifier in accordance with the rules of Classification, *i.e.* CC, UDC, DDC, LC, etc.

Example : 1m56, M8 bNo1
Annals of botany
Index to 1-10; 1887-96

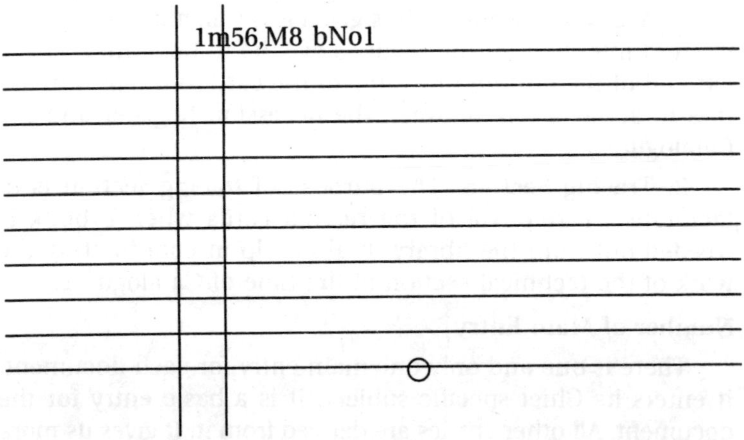

(B) Heading Section. A Heading may be the name of the person —

(a) An author

(b) A joint author

(c) A Collaborator

(d) A joint Collaborator

A heading may be a corporate body —

(a) A Government

(b) An Institution

(c) A Conference

A Heading may be geographical entity —

A Heading may be a subject

A Heading may be series and a language

Example :

HALL (James) (1755).
SINHA (Shalini) (1975).
SHARMA (CK), Ed.
CHAUDHARI (RK) and RAMKISHAN, Tr.
GODAVARY (City).
INDIA, EDUCATION (Ministry of —).
INDIA, HISTORY.
INDIA, LAW LIBRARY.
INDIA, LAW LIBRARY.
DIAGNOSIS, TUBERCULOSIS, LUNGS.

1. Person as Heading (Personal Author). It is a person of personal author, who bears responsibility for the thoughts and expression constituting the work resting solely on his *private capacity* and *Not* on the capacity of any office held in a corporate body nor on the capacity of that body.

Example : S.R. Ranganathan is the personal author of 'Five Law of Library Science' and responsible for its thoughts and Expression though he was also the President, Madras Library Association.

The person, who creates the thoughts, is taken as author.

Person as Collaborators

The person who collects and notes down the words uttered by the creator of work is regarded as Collaborator. He may be called —

(a) Editor

(b) Translator
(c) Compiler
(d) Reporter
(e) Cartographer
(f) Reviser
(g) Adapter
(h) Abridger
(i) Music-Setter (composer)

Person as Personal Authorship

1. If the title page mentions the name of persons only in author statement and does not mention or indicate the name of any corporate body, other than the one belonging to the personal trade mentioned in the imprint, the work in the document is of personal authorship.
2. The work in the document is of personal authorship,
   (a) If its primary function is the extension of the boundary of a field of knowledge or its intensification, and
   (b) The responsibility for the thoughts and expression of it rests on the person and not on the office held by him in the Corporate body in spite of being a paid or an honorary employee or a member of the corporate body.
3. A collection of learned papers or memoranda presents by person at the conference is deemed to have the respective person as author.

Different types of Personal Names (Rule HA)

The word or set of words arrange in a definite sequence and use to denote a person name of person occur in the entries of a library Catalogue. It occurs in the headings of entries as a name of an author or of a Collaborator of one kind or another.

1. The Number of words. In ancient period there were few authors and therefore, homonym among names of an author were one worded —

Homer

Kalidas

Valmiki

2. Nature of words. The essential word in the name of person are proper nouns. There are few names of persons, which includes Common Noun and auxiliary words such as article, prepositions and adjective. A serious precaution is to be taken while considering such names particularly when these are in foreign language. Proper Noun are essential in the name one or two words may denote the family Name. Common Nouns generally denotes some attributes of the person in Name of person *i.e.* Academic, Civil, Military, Ritualists, or other distinction or the profession of the person.

Specific feature of Name in Various Languages

1. Family Name at the End. In the Name of person of European, Japanese, Marathi, Gujarati, Sindhi, Kashmiri, Bengali, Oriya and Assamese cultural group. Given name precedes it.

2. Family Name at the beginning. The family name comes first and given name come thereafter in the noun of person of Chinese, Vietnamese, Malayalam, Kannada, and Telugu Culture group.

3. Given Name as last Proper Noun. The last Proper Noun is usually the Noun specification in the individual in the name of Persons of Tamil, Malayalam, Kannada, Telugu, Vietnamese Culture group.

4. Tamil Names. The preceding proper nouns may be the—

(a) Names of father, then

(b) Place of birth, or

(c) Place of ancestors.

5. Hindi Names. Given Name alone occurs without any other proper nouns.

or

Caste Names are preceded to given name.

or

Few Proper nouns based on profession or work or culture are also preceded the family name (Given Name) —

RAMDAS
RAMESH CHANDRA *SHARMA*
RAMESWAR *BHARTIYA*

Family Name

Word or word group normally is inherited by a person denoting the name of his family. It consists of proper noun. It is also denoted by the terms Surname and Last name.

Family names are of two kinds —

Word or word-group used as part of the names. There are given names after which a word or word group made of common noun are attached and cannot be removed, such word or word groups are to be used with the given name.

Example :

Ravi Bhusan
Ram Bhusan
Ram Deen
Brij Kishore
Ram Devi

Word or word-group not used as part of the name. There are few word or word group made of Common Noun or Adjectives and attached with the family name as honorific or courtesy terms after, before or in the middle of the name, such word or word group should be omitted or removed.

Example :

Baba Hari Dev
Rai Sahib Mahendar Singh
Jathedar Ramnik Singh
Kumari Rameshwari
Azhar Ali *Moulvi*
Sardar Amrinder Singh
Swami Ram Tirth

Abbreviation Word

If the proper noun in a name is not fully spelt out but abbreviation to one or more initial letter, in public usage or reference or in title page such abbreviated words are to be used as it is given on the title page.

Example :

C K Sharma	–	Chandra Kant Sharma
R P Sood	–	Ram Prasad Sood
A J Wells	–	Allen James Wells
J C Bose	–	Jagdish Chand Bose

Compound Family Name

Family name made up of two or more proper Nouns, either

1. Connected by a hyphen – or
2. Connected by a conjunction – or
3. Written separately without any connecting Symbol – or auxiliary word.

Example :

Deepak Das Gupta

A T Quillar - Couch

Surendra Nath Basu *Rai Chaudhary*

Roger Martin *Du Gard*

6

SINGLE AUTHOR

Person as Heading (MAIN ENTRY)

A name of person has to be rendered in the heading of Main Entry.

Divide the name of Personal author in three parts —

1. Entry Element. The last part or caste part or the part which is attached to given name should be put as Entry Element. If there is no such part put the given name as Heading.

If there is Entry element it will be written as under —

(a) From Second vertical or Second Paragraph or the next line where the Call Number end.

(b) It is written in Capital letter in bold upright hand and detached from one another.

Example :

CHAKRAVERTI

SHARMA

SRIVASTAVA

KHAN

SINGH

2. Secondary Element. The Secondary Element is to be the rest of the words other than the Entry Element. After the Entry Element, write the Secondary element in —

(a) Circular bracket

(b) Ordinary hand

(c) First letter in capital

(a) The sequence of the word as their occurrence in their title page.

(b) Initial letter of each word should be in capital.

(c) After the end of the Circular bracket, put a full stop.

3. Individualising Element. Individualising element is given if there are informations required to individualise the Personal author in case of homonyms such as if there are personal author of similar names and it needs separate identification

SRIVASTAVA (RAMESH).

SRIVASTAVA (RAMESH) (1937).

In above names, an individualisation element is to be put by —

(a) Date of birth

(b) Date of death

(c) Individualising element will be put in circular bracket. It will be separated by Circular bracket other than the secondary element.

(d) There will be no sign or symbols or full stop in between two circular brackets.

(e) A dash will be put to separate the date of death.

(f) If there is date of birth given only and date of death is not known or the author is alive then only the date of birth will be given in square bracket.

(g) A full stop is put at the end of the paragraph or after Circular bracket.

Example :

SHARMA (CHANDRA KANT) (1937).

RANGANATHAN (Shiyali Ramamrit) (1892-1972).

If forename or given name is given in abbreviations in title page

If the name of the personal author is given in abbreviations then —

(a) abbreviation as Secondary element

(b) Do not put any full stop in between abbreviations

Example :

SHARMA (CK).

VERMA (AK).

RANGANATHAN (SR).

Note

If there is no Personal Author the name of the Person is given on the title page or its overflow pages, find out the name out of the Reference Sources, so that it may help the reader and publishers.

One-worded Name

If the name of the Personal Author is in one word given in title page, enter under one word.

Example :

KALIDAS

VALMIKI

TULSIDAS

HOMER

DILIP KUMAR

If there are abbreviations given in Entry element, is to write the fully spelt out word as the Entry element and to write the expansion of the initial as the Secondary element.

Example :

Sri.... (Spelled out word is Srivastava)

Enter – SRI.... (*i.e.* Srivastava)

Multi-worded Name

Such names will be rendered as per above rules of elements —

1. Entry Element
2. Secondary Element
3. Individualising Element

Example :

ADAMS (Mary)(1898)

PRINCE – PATTISON (Andrew Seth) (1856-1931)

DAS GUPTA (Sachidulal) (1912)

KHAN (Mohammed Isaqullah)

7

Two Authors

If the title page contains the name of two and only two joint authors as Personal names, both the names are to be used as the Heading with the conjunction then, as under —

(a) First author (Surname / Forename) or (Entry Element / Secondary Element) (Individualising Element)

(b) 'and'

(c) Second author (Surname / Forename) or (Entry Element / Secondary Element) (Individualising Element)

Example :

SRINIVASAN (GA) and KRISHNAMACHARI (C).

SHARMA (CK) and DAVE (RK).

HARKNESS (James) and MORLEY (Frank).

Two Authors

Call Number

SRINIVASAN (GA) and KRISHNA

MACHARI (C).

8

Three or More Authors

If the title page contains the names of three or more Joint Authors (or more than two authors), the name of the first mention author alone is to be used as the Heading and the word 'and others' is to be added thereafter.

(Ranganathan says that a reader remember two names generally and two authors are usually referred to by the names of two authors and by not more than two authors, *i.e.* 'Jather & Beri', 'Ray and Sharma', 'Harkness & Morley'. Hence denied the name of three authors.)

Example :

Three or more authors

	Call Number	
		SHARMA (Chandrakant) (1937) and others.

9

PSEUDONYM AUTHOR

It is a author which assumes a false or fictitious name or any other specification different from the real name. A pseudonym may also be given by others to an author or it may even get started in a usual way, in his own time or in later times.

There are many *reasons* of keeping Pseudonym name —

(a) Diffidence

(b) Sense of Shame

(c) Fear of Consequences

(d) Freakishness

(e) Joking

(f) Mistifying

(g) Hoaxing instinct, etc.

For example :

1. Ranganathan used two Pseudonym names in his different two articles — 'Arithmeticus' in the article published in Education Review of Madras in 1922 and the other Pseudonym name 'Libra' in article contributed to 'Hindu' newspaper of Madras in 1931.

   Example :

   Arthur Travers Crowford — as TC Arthur

   Eduard Hamibtor Aitkeu — as Eha

2. A single Pseudonym may be used to represent two or more Joint author or a double Pseudonym may be used to represent a single author, producing the illusion of Join authorship.

   Example : (1) Zangwil and L Cowen — Used Jointly a Pseudonym 'J Freeman Bell'

A Pseudonym, not having the structure of a name - of - person, is to be written as it occurs on the title page of the document, without any permutation of the element constituting it.

If the title page gives only a pseudonym in the place of the author's name, the pseudonym is to be followed by the Descriptive Element '*Pseud*' e.g. —

(a) Write the name in ink on the Second Line beginning at the Second Vertical.

(b) Write in Capital letters.

Entry Element

1. First — the last word in the name.
2. After word — Secondary element in Circular Bracket and write then in ordinary hand. If initial, write in Capital letters.
3. Put comma after the Secondary element.
4. Descriptive element 'Pseud'.
5. Underline the Descriptive element.
6. Put full stop at the end of thc Section.

	Call Number	
		WESTERFIELD (JB), *Pseud.*

Pseudonym with Real name = (Individualising Element)

1. If the title page gives a Pseudonym name in place of author's name and the real name, and the real name is also given in the title page or overflow page in a

subordinate manner in a title page or in other form in a book. The Real name of the author is to be added in Circular bracket after the descriptive element 'Pseud' and a 'Comma' as under —

(a) Circular bracket starts

(b) Symbol 'i e'

(c) The Real name of the author in natural sequence in ordinary hand.

(d) Circular bracket closed.

Example :

TWAIN (Mark), Pseud, (i e Samuel Longhorne).

NIRALA, Pseud, (i e Surya Kant Tripathi).

PREMCHAND, Pseud, (i e Dhanpat Rai).

2. If the title page gives the Real name of the author and Pseudonym name is given in subordinate manner, the Real name is to be chosen for the Heading. The Pseudonym name is to be added to it and enclosed in circular brackets.

Example :

CLEMENS (Samual Longhorne), (i e Mark Twain, *Pseud*).

TRIPATHI (Surya Kant), (i e Nirala, *Pseud*).

RAI (Dhanpat), (i e Premchand, *Pseud*).

3. Real name from outside of the book —

If the Real name is not given in title page or its overflow page in the book and taken from outside sources, it will be written in Square Bracket. The same rule of Square bracket is applied for Pseudonym Name, if taken from outside sources.

Example :

P Sri, *Pseud,* [i e PS Srinivasachari].

SRINIVASACHARI (PS), (i e P Sri, *Pseud*).

Call Number

NIRALA, Psued, [i e Surya Kant Tripathi].

Call Number

CLEMENS (Samual Longhorne), (i e Mark Twain, Pseud).

10

ANONYMOUS WORK

The work of Unknown authorship is called Anonymous work either Personal author or Corporate author.

Many of the Sacred books are anonymous. Some classics are also anonymous. In other words it is a document without Author Statement.

1. The title page of an Anonymous work if it may not given the name of any collaborators. It generally happens in case of Reference sources or the work which is famous or known with its name not by its Collaborators.

   Example :

   Anglo-Assamese Dictionary / the most up to date dictionary, 10th edition. Revised and Enlarged / 1965.

   P111, J;4'k 158N65
   ANGLO-ASSAMESE (Dictionary
   etc). Ed 10.

2. *Anonymous work with Collaborators.* If the title page do not contain the author or author statement, but the

title page contains the Collaborator, such as Editor, translator etc. Choose the name of the Collaborator as the heading. Write it in ink on the second vertical. Write in Capital letters the Entry Element (*i.e.* the last word in the name) and therefore Secondary Element for the rest of word, in circular bracket. The Entry will be as under —

1. Entry Element of the name of collaborator *i.e.* Surname.
2. Secondary Element of the name of Collaborator *i.e.* Forename.
3. Comma.
4. Description Element, *i.e.*, ed., tr. etc.
5. Underline the description element.
6. Put full stop at the end of the section.

R66.6 N32

MUKHARJI (Dhana Gopal), Tr.

Song of God.

11

TITLE

1. Title. Title means Name of Work (Book).

Example : Dr. C.K. Sharma / Handbook of UGC Net.

In this example 'Hand book of UGC Net' is a title

Title may be in following kinds —

2. Subtitle. It is a Secondary or Subordinate title usually explanatory, and forming a part of the title.

Example : Heading and canons: Comparative study of five Catalogue Code / by Dr. S.R. Ranganathan.

In this example :

Main title — Headings and Canons

Sub title — Comparative study of five Catalogue Codes.

3. Alternative Title. It is a title other than main title, having equivalent place or importance and forming part of the title or introduced by 'or', is called alternative title. These are also known as Parallel title.

Example : Mahatma Gandhi or BAPU / By JL Nehru.

In this example both the title are of equivalent importance hence parallel title.

4. Short title or Abbreviated title. When a full title is given a brief or short title without any intention, prejudice, it is called short or abridged title. It is shaped or shorted intelligibly and help in identifying the work.

Generally speaking, initial words other than an article — such as, Element, Hand book, Introduction, primer, treatise — may have to be preserved.

Example :

UNO	–	United Nations Organization
ILA	–	Indian Library Association
INSDOC	–	Indian National Scientific Documentation Center
CCC	–	Classified Catalogue Code
AACR–II	–	Anglo-American Cataloguing Rules–II

5. Half title. Half title is always put on the page of printed book, usually before the page containing the full title of the work contained in the book.

Half title page	Title Page
AACR-II	Anglo-American Cataloguing Rules-II

6. Uniformised title. When the title is uniformised by —

(a) Popular

(b) Cataloguing usage in lieu of listless

(c) Often unintended

  (a) Varients of the title of one and the same work indifferent editions.

  (b) Title of different volumes of one and the same work.

  Example :

  Code civil des Francais — Later titled as 'Code Napolean'

  Bible

  Vedas

  Administrative report on agriculture (in 1998)

  Annual report on agriculture (in 1999)

7. Fanciful title. Title that does not disclose the subject of the work.

Example : Meghaduta

8. Title proper of Periodical Publications. It includes the name of the sponsor if it occurs at the beginning and excludes it if it occurs at the end.

Example :

Aslib Proceedings

Library Association record

Annuals of the Indian Library Association

Rules for Title Entry

(1) Language — Language of the library

(2) Initials — Initial articles are to be omitted

(3) Honorifics — Honorifics are to be omitted

(4) Title words — Title words are to be arranged / written in the sequence in which they occur in the Title page.

Examples :

The BIBLE = BIBLE

The Life of Johnson = Life of Johnson

SRIMAD BHAGAVATAM = BHAGAVATAM

When Title Entry needed

Title Entry is allowed only in a case where the title is Fanciful and almost amounts to proper name for a book. Such a title does not usually indicate the subject of the book. If the Title is fairly descriptive of the subject of a book or indicates it to some extent, the title is denied the privilege of contributing an entry of the book.

One reason for this is that the subject entry of the book, derived directly from its subject itself, will serve the purpose better.

Further a descriptive title is usually flabby, verbose, and without a proper focal word — called 'catch word' (in German Practice) at its beginning.

Entry Element

When the Title occurs in the heading the first two words are to be deemed to form the Entry Element.

LIFE of Samuel Johnson.
By Allen. 0,4y7K52

Puff

In rendering the title in the Title section or in the Heading of a main entry, if there is any PUFF, at the middle or at the end of the Title, it is to be omitted and is to be replaced by three dots (...) if in the middle. And replace by 'etc', if in the end.

Examplc :

1. Verbose Title – (in Main Entry).

   Travels into East India and Arabia Deserts ... in familiar letter to his friend Srgnior Marie Sehipano.

2. A plain Treatise on; an <u>exact and full</u> account.

   = A treatise on; an account.

3. Omit dcscriptivc words —

   Compendious pocket dictionary

   = Compendious dictionary

   Or

   Pocket Dictionary.

Short Title

While rendering the title in main entry or in Heading Section (Book Index Entry) or in Cross Reference Entry, the Short Title is to be used; and the words in it are to be written in the sequence in which they occur in the Title Page.

Individualising Element

If the two or more Book Index Entries have the same title as Heading and if the Homonym is not resolved by the Second Section, the Individualising Element is to in the Sequence of preference to resolve the Homonyms.

1. Author, if the name of the author is known.
2. Year of its first publication, if the year is known.
3. Name of the Version.
4. Class to which it belongs.

Example :

GENESIS (Anglo-Saxon poems).

GENESIS (Old-Saxon poems).

12

EDITION

First Edition of a work is never considered for entry.

Edition means "one of the different printing or reproductions of a document with or without slight change in thought–content each being distinguished from the others, either numerically or by some other equivalent term such as 'New', 'Revised' and 'Enlarged'."

Edition is also considered of such works which have one or the different form in which one and the same work is published, each form having a distinctive name almost amounting to a proper noun — such as "Arden Edition", "Classic Edition", 'Variorum Edition', and "Centenary Edition" etc.

In view of the above, the following change occur in the revised edition —

1. Different printing of the work/document
2. Different reproduction of the work/document
3. Slight change in thought Contents of the work
4. Distinguished with the previous document,
   (a) Numerically
   (b) or by some other equivalent term
5. Different form in which one and the same work is published.
6. Each form having a distinction name almost amounting a proper noun.

Edition Statement

It includes —

(a) Specific feature of edition

(b) The word 'Ed'

(c) Number of Edition

1. Record the number of each of the successive edition or of a distinctive editions of the work or document with a proper name, along with the year of publication of each.
2. Information regarding edition is to be given only in case of the second the later edition having special names.
3. If the edition is to be described numerically, the appropriate number is to be written after the word 'Ed'.
4. If the edition has a special name, initial article and honorific word, if any, are to be omitted.

   Example :

   Centenary ed.
5. If an Edition is with Distinctive Name, it is rendered as under —

   (a) Name of the author;

   (b) Comma; and

   (c) Name of the Edition

   Example :

   Sankara, memorial ed.

   Shakespeare (William), Variorum ed.

   Tolstoy (Leo), Centenary ed.

0,111, 2J64, 0M86

SHAKESPEARE (William).

Othello. New Variorum ed 11.

312

C&dE N56

HAMILL (John Bernard).

Difference between Physics and Chemistry. Ed 2.

212

13

COLLABORATORS

The Person associated with a work and/or its author or author in a secondary capacity not amounting to authorship, or The Person who is not author or among the author but works as author in a Secondary Capacity, is called Collaborator/s.

i.e.	Director,	Reviser,
	Guide,	Editor,
	Assistant,	Reporter,
	Commentator,	Foreword,
	Illustrator,	Epitomiser,
	Engraver,	Adopter,
	Translator,	Libratist,
		Writer or Composer of Music,
		Writer of pictorial work.

Example :

Manual of Chemical technology by RV Wagner and revised by F. Fischer.

Main author — RV Wagner

Collaborator — Fischer (F), Reviser.

1. The Entry of collaborator is a third part of the Title Section — Title — Edition — Collaborators.
2. Collaborator are mention / written / in title section with its Pure Name or Name in natural sequence without any change or permutation of the words in the name.
3. The name of Collaborator is written with its designation. The designation will be written in the beginning of the name with words by added to it.

Example : Ed by RK Mohenty
Tr by CK Sharma
Rev by PK Ghosh

4. If there are two Collaborators of any one kind of Collaborators, both the names are to be written out.
5. If there is a mention of the statement 'Rev ed' in the Collaborator Statement on the title page, put it in square brackets after the title. At the end of Edition Statement put a Full stop. Then add of the description word 'Rev'. Then add "by." Put the full stop at the end of the section.

Example 1 : Main Entry

	V	N28
		DATTA (DN)
		History. [Rev ed]. Rev by
	A	L Srivastava.
	215	

Example 2 : Reviser Index Entry

	SRIVASTAVA (AL), Rev.	
		Datta : History. [Rev ed]. V N28

6. If there are <u>two Collaborators</u> of the same kind, put them in Collaborator statement in Title section in the same sequence in which they occur. Put 'and' in between them.

Example : (Two translators)

```
        B N32
          KLEIN (Felix).
          Elementary mathematics. Tr from
        the German by ER Hedrick and
        CA Noble.




        541
```

7. If there are <u>three or more Collaborators</u> of same kind, put them in Collaborator Statement in Title Section in the same sequence in which they occur. Write or mention the name of the first Collaborator and add 'and others' after it.

```
        CN37
          MOHIT KUMAR and VERMA
        (P N).
          Elements of physics. Assis by
        AC Grover and others.
```

8. If there are two or more kinds of collaborators, write them in the sequence they occur, *i.e.*

   (a) Designation of the first kind of collaborator

(b) add 'by' with the designation.

(c) Name of the first kind of collaborators

(d) 'Semicolon' (to connect two kinds of collaborators)

(e) Designation of the second kind of collaborator — 'Ed', 'Tr'

(f) add 'by' with the designation, 'Ed by', 'Tr by'.

(g) Name of second kind of collaborator

(h) If there are third kind of collaborators the same rules will be applied as in case of two kinds of collaborators.

	C	NO5
		GANOT (AL) and LONE (E).
		Natural philosophy. Ed 4. Tr by
	E	James and PK Rogers; rev by
	AW	Reinold and Georg Allen.
	51	

14

Note Section

It is a section of the main Entry giving an Annotation, or a Synopsis, or an abstract of the document Catalogued.

There are many kind of Notes —

1. Series Note and Multiple Series Note
2. Extract and Extraction Note
3. Change of Title Note
4. Associated Book Note

1. Series Note. There are many opinions about a Series Note. In fact experiences goes to prove the importance of the series. The Statement in the main Entry showing that the book belongs to a particular series, is found to be sufficient for most purpose, *i.e.*

(a) Where Subjects are so various as to have no unity.

(b) If there is no relation to one another subject.

(c) Or characteristics are common.

(d) Where the various volumes are more or less akin or connected in subject though it is seldom that people want to read through a series systematically or wish to know what volumes are contain in it.

If there are more than one note, the sequence will be — Series Note, Multiple Series Note, Extract Note, Change of Title Note, Extraction Note and Associated Book Note.

Each Note will be written separately.

Rendering

(a) There should be a set sequence among the Note if more than one.

(b) All Notes should be written separately.

(c) Note should start from the Second vertical.

(d) Continuation will be from first vertical.

(e) Note will have its number in the end.

(f) Series Note will be written in circular brackets.

(g) Other Note will be clubbed in inverted commas, *e.g.* Extract and Extraction Note.

15

Series Note

A Series Note has three parts —

1. Series —
    (a) Main Series,
    (b) Sub series
2. Editor-of-Series
3. Number of Series

All above parts will be written in the same sequence.

1. Series Note —
    (o) A Series Note will be clubbed in circular brackets.
    (a) Name of the Series. Initial articles and Honorific word if any will be omitted.
    (b) Sub series or subordinate series. It will be Connected by colon ' : '
    (c) Slash
    (d) The word 'Ed by'

SERIES

It is a set of book, not constituting a multi volumed book, and with the following attributes :

1. The books are issued, normally successively by one publisher or by one sponsoring body or person, usually in a uniform style, and having some similarity of Subject or standard or purpose;
2. Each book has normally a distinct and independent title and/or other feather of its oven;
3. Each book has normally a different author;

4. There is a collective name to denote the set, called the 'Name of the book of the books of the set'; and
5. Each book is or can be assigned a distinct number called the Serial Number. It may belong to a system of Simple or complex, ordinal number such as 1,2,3 etc..., 3.1, 3.2, 3.3; etc or 1957.1, 1957.2, 1957.3 etc.

   Example : Classified Catalogue Code.

   1. Ranaganathan Series in Library Science 2.
   2. University of Delhi, Library Science Series.
   3. Modern World Series.

The name of a series may have to be rendered in the Note Section of a Main Entry.

If the Name of a series occurs in variant forms in several pages of a book or in several books of the series, that which gives the maximum information in the shortest form is to be used as the Uniformised Name for rendering.

If the Name of a Series does not occur anywhere in a book but occur in some other book of the series, it is to be taken from that book.

If the Name of the Series is not individualising.

For example :

English Series

Publication Series

Translation Series

Its name is to be preceded by the name of an individualising Entry with which it is associated — such as —

Publisher

Sponsor

University

Followed by a comma ' , '

Example :

Madras Library Association, bibliographical series, Patna University, readership series.

University of Delhi, Library Science series.

Editor

(a) The Name of the Editor/s of the series

(b) A full stop

(c) The Series Number

(d) Circular bracket closed.

(e) A full stop.

Editor of Series

The Name of Editor will be written in Nature Sequence and in ordinary hand.

If there are two Editors, both the Editors will be written connected by Conjunction 'and'. But if more than two editors, connect by conjunction 'and others'.

Serial Number

(a) The serial is to be the Number indicating the position of the book in the series, as is given by the publisher.

(b) If the publisher has not assigned Serial Number, the books are to be given Serial Numbers in the Sequence of the Accession or in any other Convenient Sequence.

(c) It will be more appropriate if the Serial Number may be replaced by a year or a year and a number or any other similar entity appropriate to the book.

Serial number may be rendered as under —

1. Serial number of the Series (Series Number) is by fullstop ' . '
2. Series Number as given in the title page in figures in Indo Arabic numerals. If the Series Number is given in words or in roman, it is to be translated in to Arabic numbers 1, 2, 3, 4, ... 9, 10, 11, ... 19, 20, 21, ... 29 and so on.
3. Enclosed the Section by the Circular bracket.
4. Put full stop at the end of the section, after brackets.

B 111 N10
SINGHANIA (Laxman).
Elementary Arithmatics and
Algebra. Ed 3.
(Mathematical series.7).

33

T N32
VERMA (RK) and SINHA (SN).
Dynamics of education.
(International library of
Psychology and Scientific method.
Ed by CK Saxena and Mukesh
Agrawal.29).

81

Three or more editors

B N14
SHARMA (SK).
Introduction to mathematics:
a number game. Ed 2.
(Home library of modern knowledge.
Ed by Ramendra Misra and others. 5).

517

INDEPENDENT SERIES

Each Independent series note is to be written in separate sections. A book may belong to two or more series. Each series is said to be independent, if the individualisation of the name of one is independent of the name of the other. Each Independent Series will begin from Second Vertical.

V4475 N31
MUKHARJI (Ronit).
History of Bengal. Ed 3.
(University of Calcutta, Publications.
116).
(Jadavpur University, historical
Series.21).

76

ALTERNATIVE NAMES SERIES AND DEPENDENT SERIES

Alternative name of series means the series with two or more names. The primary series has two alternative names.

The Alternative names series are to be written as under —

0. The circular bracket open.
1. The first series
2. The word 'or'
3. The second (Alternate Series)
4. Full stop
5. The Number
6. Semi colon ';' (if any dependent or sub series of both the Alternative Name Series)
7. The Name of dependent or sub series.
8. Full stop
9. Number

10. Circular bracket closed
11. Full stop.

O,	15,1 D40, M N31
	KALIDAS.
	Meghduta, with commentaries.
Ed	by NS Khiste.
	(Kashi Sanskrit Series or
Haridas Sanskrit Granthmala.88;	
Kavya Section.14).	
95	

Dependent series is also known as Interdependent series. It is to be rendered as under —

1. Primary Series
2. Number of Primary Series
3. Semi colon ';'
4. The Name of Secondary Series
5. A Full stop
6. Number of the Secondary Series
7. A Semi colon ';'
8. The Name of the Ternary Series
9. A Full Stop
10. Number of the ternary series.

It is not necessary that every series have its number. It may or may not. The number in any series will be written with the related series to which the number belongs.

	S;	811 N32
		WESTERFIELD (JB).
		Scientific dream book and
	dictionary of symbols. Ed 2.	
		(University of London, bulletin.
	19; science series; studies in	
	Symbols. 10).	

Author Name as Individualising Element

If the Entity used for individualising a series is the author of the book, the name of the Individualising Entity is to be replaced by the term 'Its' 'His' or 'her' in italic or underline, in the Series Note of the Main Entry.

	B	N14
		WHITEHEAD (AN).
		Introduction to Mathematics.
		(Its selective papers. 35).

Major and Minor Series

If the Name of a Series consists of two distinct parts — *viz* those donating a Major Series and Minor Series is not sufficient to individualise it, the rendering is to consist successively of the name of the Major Series, a comma, and the Name of the Minor Series.

Example :

Tagore Lectures (University of Shanti Niketan).

Nirala Lectures (University of Allahabad).

Pseudonym Series

It is of three types —

1. The Series of the book not constituting a multi-volume books but of common authorship, of the same edition and the title of distinctive part in addition to the name of edition.
2. Series of a set of books not constituting a multi-volume books but of common authorship, having a common part used their common generic title, each book having distinctive part, each book is assigned a Series Number of Simple and Complex ordinal numbers.
3. A set of books not constituting a multi-volumed books but not having a common authorship, the title of all books having a common part using a common generic title, and each title of book having a distinctive part using a common generic title, each book having a distinctive part using a common generic title, and each title of book having a distinctive part using a common generic title, each book assigning a serial Number of a system of simple and complex ordinal Numbers.

DIFFERENCE BETWEEN PSEUDO SERIES

Type-I	Type-II	Type-III

Common Feature : A set of books not constituting a Multi-Volume book.

Type-I	Type-II	Type-III
1. Books of common authorship	Books of common authorship	Books of common authorship
2. Books belong to the same edition	Titles of the books have a common part being used as their common generic title	Titles of books having a common part used as a common generic title
3. Title of each book has a	Title of each book is different but having	Title of each book has a distinctive

distinctive part in addition to the name of the edition.	a common generic title.	part of its own in addition to a generic part.
4. Each book is assigned a serial number by a system of ordinal numbers.	Each book is assigned a serial number by a system or ordinal numbers.	Each book can be assigned a serial number by a system of ordinal number.
5. Each edition having a name of author being used as a name of the Series.	The name of the author taken along with the generic title suitable to be used as if a name of a series.	The generic title is used suitably as if it were a name of the series.
Example : (Shakespeare [William]. New Variorum Ed. Ed. By HH Furness.7)	*Example* : (Ramanna [E]. Text-book of Physics Ed. By R. Shivraman.5)	*Example* : (Hunt [William] and Poole [RL]. Ed. Political history of England.4).

THESIS SERIES

Publication of theses (of any discipline or degree) submitted to a University or any other body are to be deemed to belong to a series, whose name is to consist successively of the following :

1. The name of the university or any other body
2. Comma ','
3. The word 'theses'
4. Full stop
5. The Year
6. Comma ','
7. Serial Number of 'theses' of the year: If it is a research thesis, the Year of thesis is given. In absence of other informations it is marked as the Serial Number of these presented in a particular year.

4.44'N7 N66

BISNOI (RN).

Journalism in India.

(University of Bombay, thesis.

1967, 1).

129

16

Extract Note

A document which embodies a portion of another document.

When a part of a Host Work Document is separately published as a book or Extract, referring the Host document, a Extract Note is to be given in Note Section.

An Extract Note is to consist successively of the —

1. *Descriptive words* "Extract from" or "supplement to" as the case may be or other appropriate ones; and
2. Brief specification of the work from which it is extracted.
3. Descriptive words are to be underlined, if written in hand script.
4. The Extract Note is to be put within inverted commas.
5. A full stop is put after the inverted closed at the end of the Note.

2,2.44; (Z'q) N31
RANGANATHAN (SR).
Model Public Library Act.
(Madras Library Association, Legislative
Series. 1).
"**<u>Extract from</u>**
T'm44,N2 N30
South Indian Teacher, (South India
Teachers' Union). 3;1930; 548-556".

EXTRACT FROM PERIODICALS

If the extract is from a periodical Publication, the information given in 'Extract Note' is to consist of —

1. Call No. of the volume of the Periodical
2. The Name of the Periodical Publication
3. A colon : and
4. The term 'V'; and
5. The number or the year or both of the volume of the Periodical Publication, the number and the year being separated by a semi-colon,

OR

Any other appropriate specification of the locus.

Example : Extract from a Periodical

2,7362, d N21
SWANTON (W 1) (1869), Comp.
Libraries in District of Columbia.
(National Research Council, reprint
and circular series. 20).
"Extract from Special Libraries.
V12;1921".

54855

It is of two kinds —

1. Extract from a book
2. Extract from periodical

EXTRACT FROM A BOOK

If it is a Extract from a book the Entry will consist of —

1. Call Number of the book
2. Heading of the book
3. A Full stop
4. A short title of the Extract book

5. The first word of the title beginning with Capital Letters
6. A Full stop; and
7. The parts, Chapters of pages of the host book
8. If Heading is the title, the above serial 2, 3 are to be omitted.

2: (Z44) qN57
RANGANATHAN (Shiyali Ramamrita)
(1892).
Union Library Act.
"Extract from Ranganathan
(Shiyali Ramamrita) 1892. Five
Laws of Library Science. Ed 2. Sec. 43".

40003

17

EXTRACTION NOTE

The Extract Note is given in the Host documents from which Extract is taken.

Example :

1. Main book (Host Document)	=	Library Management and organisation / by Dr. C.K. Sharma
2. Extract of the host document (*i.e.* one chapter of the book is extracted and published separately)	=	"Nature and Size of Staff". Chapter 5 Pages 26-43 of the host document 'Library Management and Organisation' by Dr. C.K. Sharma

The information to be given in Extraction Note will consist of —

1. Directing word "For extract see"
2. Heading of the Extract
3. Title of the Extract
4. Information of the Edition, if other than Edition!
5. Extraction Note will be a Separate Section in the Note Section starting from the Second Vertical.

	2	8 N83
		SHARMA (CK) (1937).
		Library Management and Organization. V 1.
		"For extracts see
		2:8 N83 SHARMA (CK) (1937).
	N	ature and size of staff".
	23	1

CHANGE OF TITLE

If the Name of a book is changed and published with other name, a Note Section of the book of Changed Name will consist of the following entry specifications —

1. Directing words — "Published previously as" or 'published later as' or 'Published in India as' ('Published in ...... as' Note is given to such books which are published in other countries other than the favoured Country, with Change Name).
2. Each of the title under which it has appeared.
3. 'The change of title Note' is to be put written inverted commas.

	2	N82
		SHARMA (CK).
		History of Library Science.
		"Published previously as
		Development of library science".
	34	3

	T	OgY
		RUSSEL (Bertrand).
		Education and the social order.
		"Published in USA as
		Education and the modern world".
	109	

There are other related phrases indicating the nature of 'Change of Names' as follows —

1. "For an associated book".
2. "For an abridgement".
3. "For a merger book".
4. "For a merged book".

18

Accession Number

Accession Number Section

1. Last section in the front of a Main Entry Card, giving the Accession Number of the document.
2. The Accession Number section is to begin at the First Vertical of the bottom-most line of the Card.
3. If two or more Accession Numbers are to be in a sequence parallel to that of the Book Number to which they correspond.
4. The Accession Number is to be taken from the back of the title page.
5. If there is no title page for a document the Accession Number is to be taken from the top of the first page.
6. It is assigned by the Accessioner, the person who Accession the book in Accession Register.

2:8 N91
SHARMA (CK).
Library Administration. Ed 2. Tr from
the German by ER Hedrick and
CA Noble.

235

7. Accession Number is a Serial Number which indicates the serial number of the book in a Accession Register entered in Continuous Sequence of the Serial Number.

Ranganathan says that the provision for entering the Accession Number in the Fifth Section of the Main Entry is, no doubt, unusual. It is not intended for the Reader's eye. It is to be written at the left end of the bottom-most line of the reader to minimum. The reason for inserting it at all is purely administrative. It is to act as a link between the Accession Register and the Catalogue.

19

TRACING SECTION

It is given on the back of the Main entry card, indicating all the Added Entries of the document. Tracing Section is not generally given in a catalogue in Book form. (Rule. FQ)

The purpose of the Tracing Section is to facilitate the removal of all the related cards, when a book is weeded out from the library. This is of use to the Maintenance Section. It is also of help in coordinating the work of the Technical Section at the time of Cataloguing. Some enter the Tracing Section in a separate slip called Process Slip. (Rule. MB)

The following informations are furnished in the Tracing Section. Such information is related to additional entries made for the book —

1. Cross Reference Entry
2. Class Index Entry
3. Cross Reference Index Entry

Structure of Tracing Section

Tracing Section (on back of the Main Entry) is divided with Imaginary lines may be drawn by a sharp edge of the ordinary pencil.

1. It is to be divided into two halves drawn parallel to its shorter sides.
2. Two halves are called — 'Left Half' and
   'Right Half' respectively
   Left side is called 'Left Half'
   Right side is called 'Right Half'
3. *The Right half* is divided into three convenient parts as per the space engaged by the entries or the number of entries.

Imaginary lines are drawn at convenient distances parallel to the longer sides of the card. The parts are called —

(a) Upper part

(b) Middle part

(c) Lower part

(a) Upper Part of Right Half (Rule. MH5). In this part the Headings of the Class Index Entries, contributed by the Chains of the Class Number of the book and of the Cross Reference Entries, beginning from the last link and ending with the Uppermost link.

(b) Middle Part of Right Half (MH6). The Middle part is to contain successively the heading of each of the Book Index Entries of the book, in the sequence in which they are treated. (Rule. MJ)

(c) Lower Part of Right Half (MH7). The Lower Part is to contain successively the Heading of each of the Cross Reference Index Entries of the book in the sequence in which they are treated. (Rule. ML)

Example 1 : Tracing Section (Back of the main entry)

'LEFT HALF' 'RIGHT HALF'

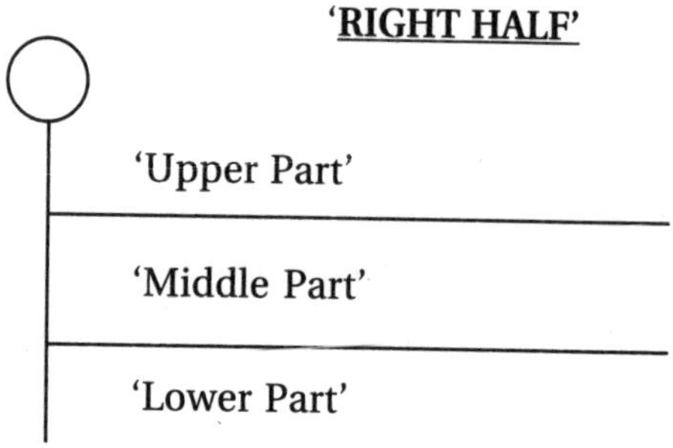

Example 2 :

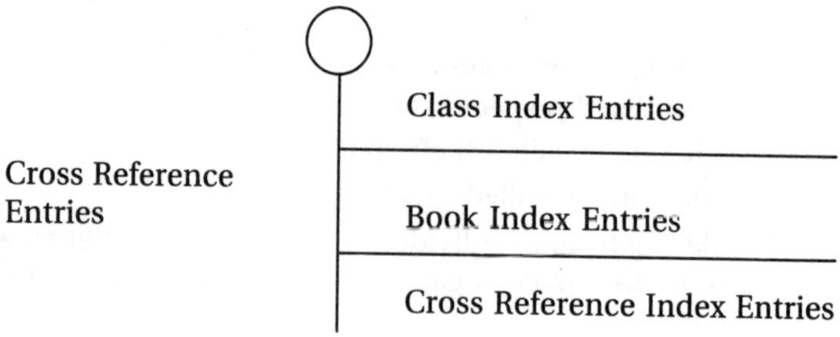

MAIN ENTRY

O,15, 2 D40, SN22
KALIDASA.
Sakuntala. Ed 2. Ed by R Pischel.
(Harvard Oriental series. Ed by
CR Laxman. 16).

174

Class Index Entries by Chain procedure

Class Number – 0, 15, 2D40, S – Sakuntala

CHAIN

0	= Literature (Sought Link)
0,	= Connecting Symbol (False Link)
0,1	= Indo-European Literature (Unsought Link)
0,15	= Sanskrit Literature (Sought Link)
0,15,	= Connecting Symbol (False Link)
0,15,2	= Sanskrit Drama (Sought Link)
0,15,2D40	= Drama of Kalidas (Sought Link)
0,15,2D40,	= Connecting Symbol (False Link)
0,15,2D40,S	= Sakuntala (Sought Link)

Total links in Chain = 9

The link ending with a Indicator Digit are False Link.

The relevant link representing the Proper Subjects are Sought Links.

Class Index Entries represented in Tracing Section (Back of Main Entry Card)

Shakuntla. O, 15, 2D40,S
Drama, Kalidas, 0,15,2D40
Sanskrit Drama, Kalidas. 0,15,2
Sanskrit Literature, Drama,
Kalidas.0,15
Literature 0

Kalidas.
Pischel, R., Ed.
Harinand Oriental series

Lauman, CR, Ed.

Precaution

While deciding the side of Tracing Section or the angle of the card setting, it must be remembered that —

1. In passing from the front side to the back side, the card is to be turned through two right angles with the bottom edge.
2. The writing of the back of the card should begin on the first line near the bottom of the card as it stands in the cabinet tray.
3. Other lines should be written successively after it.

Left Half

One line of the left half is devoted to each Cross Reference Entry (CRE). It contains —

1. Class Number which forms the leading Section of the Cross Reference Entry; and if necessary,
2. Word "P" followed by the page of reference or the word "Sec", or "Chap", or "Part" etc. followed by the Number(s) concerned.

Example of Multifocal book

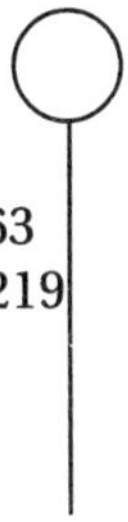

0,111,M64:g P 1-152
0,111,2J64:g P 220-263
0,111,3M67:g P 153-219

3. Cross Reference Entries generally made in case of multifocal book has many Parts or volumes or chapters etc. of different title and also different contributors / authors. Moreover a book may be turned one two or more subjects coordinated with one another, and belonging to an array which has a subjects of larger extension as their common immediate universe.

   Example :

   Main Subject of the book – Physics
   Chapters – Sound, Heat, Radiation, Electricity, and Magnetism.
   Each Chapter has a separate contributor / or author.
   The other Multifocal book is that which consists of two or more subject.

   Example :

   Main Subject of a book — Literature
   Chapters / Parts — Drama, Poetry, Prose etc.
   Each chapter / part has a separate Contributor / author.
   Main subject of the book has a common author / Contributor.

   Third multifocal book is that which has threc parts / chapters. But each part / chapter has different author / contributor. There is no necessary that that chapters / parts are necessary. There may not any mention of parts / chapters, but they may be differentiated by their title, author and pages.

   Example :

   Three studies in English Literature! A. Chevrillion (0, 111; gM7N23)

1. Poetry by Rudyard Kipling. Page 1-152.
   (Class No. 0, 111, 1M64:g)
2. Drama by John Galsworthy.
   p.153-219
   (0, 111, 3M67:g)
3. English soul by Shakespeare, p.220-263.
   (0, 111, 3M64:g)

All the above three books bound together have different subjects with different contributors/authors.

It is a Multifocal book.

Rendering

Main Entry Under —

O, 111:g M7 N23
CHEVRILLION (A).
Three studies in English Literature.
Kipling, Galsworthy, Shakespeare.
Tr from the French by F. Simmonds.

249

Cross Reference Entry from First contributor

O,111,:M64:g
See also
0,111:g M7 N23

Three studies in English literature.
P1-152.

Cross Reference Entry from Second contributor

	O,	111,3 M67:g
		See also
		0,111:g M7 N23
		Chevrillion.
		Three studies in English literature.
	P1	53-219.

Cross Reference Entry from Third contributor

	O,	111,2J64:g
		See also
		0,111:g M7 N23
		Chevrillion.
		Three studies in English literature.
	P2	20-263.

General rules of Tracing Section

1. Style of writing. All the words should be written in ordinary hand.

The first letter of each entry and the first letter of Proper Noun is to be written in Capital.

2. Continuation line. A continuation line is to be indented by two spaces, if one entry is not complete in one line.

3. Punctuation. A Full stop is to be inserted at the end of the headings.

A Full stop is to be inserted at the end of each of the Items corresponding to each Cross Reference Entry.

20

CORPORATE BODY

Corporate body means a body or bodies means a bodies United or organized, or coming together informally, in a common sense or common action such as —

1. Government bodies or organizations,
2. Commercial bodies or organizations,
3. Industrial bodies or organizations,
4. Service bodies or organizations,
5. Political bodies or organizations,
6. Deliberations bodies or organizations,
7. Collective expression of opinion or Statement.

Example :

I. Govt. of India
   Govt. of U.P. or other states
   Local Government bodies
   Other Govt. bodies like commission and commission established by the Governments

II. Institutions — which are not Government bodies.
   INTUC
   India Mathematical Society
   India Library Association of Library Associations
   Inter-University Board of India
   Commonwealth University's Conference
   State Bank of India
   Indian National Congress
   Charan Singh University
   M.M. College, Modinagar

Organ of Corporate Body

Non-Autonomous part of a corporate body or the body which has independent existence called Organ of corporate body *i.e.*

1. The constitution of parent body.
2. A legislative, executive or administrative measure, for administrative or deliberative work for an indefinite period, within the field of function of parent body.
3. A legislative executive or administrative measures for functions of parent body for —
   (a) an indefinite period
   (b) for specific piece of work for specific duration
   (c) organ intrinsic to the constitutive of the Parent body
   (d) organ of any of the first remove (organ of Source remove)
   (e) organ of any of the second remove (organ of the third remove).

Parent Body

1. First remove
2. Second remove
3. Organ of the third remove

A organ is a Subordinate body of the Parent body. It may be constitutional organ, permanent organ or temporary organ.

Govt. of India —	<u>Parent Body</u>	Ministry of Finance
	Ist organ	Department of Finance
	IInd organ	Finance Committee
	IIIrd organ	Taxation Section

Example 1 — Temporary organ —

Parent body — Government of India

Temporary organ — India Taxation Enquiry Commission, 1956

Example 2 — Government of India (Parent body)

First Remove = Lok Sabha

Second Remove = Privilege Committee

Third Remove = Advisory Committee to Privilege Committee.

Person Vs Corporate Body

(a) If the title page does not mention the Name of person(s) in the author Statement.

(b) But if the title page mention or indicates the name of corporate body other than a body belonging to the publishing trade mention in the imprint.

(c) If there is also internal evidence of corporate authorship —

The work in the document is of corporate authorship provided that —

(i) even in the case of names of the corporate body mention in the imprint being only that of a body belonging to a publishing trade.

(ii) if it is a work by the corporate body itself.

Such as — its (Corporate body's) Catalogue, administrative report, history etc.

Such work in the document is of corporate authorship.

21

GOVERNMENT

The responsibility for the thought and expression constituting a work may rest solely on a Government as a whole. The Government as a whole is taken to be the author of such a work.

If the corporate body is a government as a whole, its name is to be the name of its territory.

Example : (Form 1)

Government of India – as 'INDIA'

Government of Punjab – as 'PUNJAB'

Mysore State – as 'MYSORE'

Mysore District – as 'MYSORE (District)'

Agra city – as 'AGRA (city)'

Example : (Form 2)

Police Headquarter of Haryana in Chandigarh — as HARYANA, POLICE (Headquarter) (Chandigarh)

District Board of Meerut – as 'MEERUT (District)'

Jaipur city Municipality – as 'JAIPUR (City)'

Constitutional Organ

Constitutional organ (the name of the constitutional) organ of a Government is to be used as Second Heading as it is —

(a) Current in the language of the library.

(b) Otherwise in the language of territory concerned.

Examples :

(1) INDIA, MINISTRY

(2) GREAT BRITAIN, COUNCIL

(3) LUCKNOW, MUNICIPAL COUNCIL

(4) INDIA, COUNCIL OF MINISTERS.

Rule (for Heading)

1. Choose the name of the Government as a whole for the heading. Represent it by the name of its territory — that is, GREAT BRITAIN — only. The term to be used in the library and to be taken from a Standard Gazetteer, preference being given to an official source.
2. Write the words in the name in Capital letters in their Natural Sequence. Write all the letter in each word in a hold, up right hand, detach from one another.
3. Put a Full stop at the end of the section.

Legislature Body

Examples :

1. INDIA, RAJYA SABHA.
2. INDIA, LOK SABHA.
3. UP, LEGISLATIVE ASSEMBLY.
4. MADRAS (City), COUNCIL.
5. AGRA, DISTRICT BOARD.
6. UNITED STATES OF AMERICA, SENATE.

HEAD OF THE GOVERNMENT

The Name of the Head of a Government is used as second Heading and rendered with the name of the occupant of that office as an individualising element.

In a Government bodies/departments, and the Head of the Government is immortal (Not the person occupying the position of Head). Therefore the name of the body or the position, which is Head of Government is treated as Entry Element. On the other hand the person occupying the position as Head of the Government is considered as Secondary element.

The rendering will be as follows —

1. Geographical entity of the Government —

   i.e. INDIA for (Government of India)

   GREAT BRITAIN for (Government of Great Britain)

   UTTAR PRADESH for (Government of Uttar Pradesh)

2. Head of the Government —

   i.e. INDIA, PRESIDENT.

   USA, PRESIDENT

   BANGLADESH, PRIME MINISTER.

3. Person holding as Head of Government —

   i.e. INDIA, PERSIDENT (Rajendra Prasad)

   JAPAN, EMPEROR (Hirohito)

   UTTAR PRADESH, GOVERNOR (VK Shastri).

   MADRAS (City), MAYOR (S Satyamurty).

Attention

The kind of corporate Heading is to be used only in the case of official such as —

(a) Messages,

(b) Proclamations,

(c) Dispatches,

(d) Ordinances,

(e) Other publication emanating from the Heading of the Government.

2. This kind of Heading is not applicable to works written by a king, a president etc. in his private capacity.

   i.e. The messages read by President will be rendered —

   INDIA, PRESIDENT (V.V. Giri).

Not as

Giri (V.V.) (President).

But if book is written by the President Dr. Rajendra Prasad in his own private capacity, the rendering will be —

Example : My views on Political Scenario of Pakistan — by Dr. Rajendra Prasad.

RAJENDRA PRASAD.

My views on Political Scenario of Pakistan.

GIRI (V.V.)

Few days with Gandhi ji /

Judiciary Body

Examples :

1. INDIA, SUPREME COURT.
2. GREAT BRITAIN, COURT OF APPEAL.
3. HARYANA, HIGH COURT.
4. AGRA, CRIMINAL COURT.

All above organ (First remove) has their over name in the language of the country. They are almost proper names.

Permanent Organs

The de facto responsibility for the thought and permanent organ of a Government. The organ of the Government is taken to be the author of a such work.

Such bodies may be a —

1. Executive department or body,
2. Administrative department or body.
3. Judiciary department or body,
4. Legislative department or body,

Examples :

1. INDIA, AGRICULTURE (Department of —)
2. INDIA SUPREME COURT.
3. CHANDIGARH, MUNICIPAL (Council).
4. RAJASTHAN, MINISTERS (Council of —)
5. MYSORE (City), MUNICIPALITY.

Head of Governments

The de facto responsibility for the thought and expression constituting a work may rest solely on a Temporary organ of a Government. The organ of the Government is taken to be the author of such a work.

Subordinate Court of Law

If two or more courts of Law of the same Government have similar names, the Homonym is to be, in sequence of preference, a term denoting either :

1. The Area of Jurisdiction; or
2. The Headquarter; or
3. Any other necessary and sufficient attribute.

Example :

INDIA, DISTRICT COURT (Agra).

HARYANA, DISTRICT MAGISTRATE'S COURT (Rohtak).

PAKISTAN, CIRCUIT COURT OF APPEALS (Third Circuit).

Administrative Department

Every Government whether Nation, State or at local level has many departments such as —

1. Headquarter or the Parent Department,
2. Subordinate Department(s)
3. Though Subordinate department but they are recognised as independent entity or they are in the position to be treated as Second organ or heading.

Example : INDIA, EDUCATION (Commission) Education Commission may have its Parent body *i.e.* Ministry of Education.

Administrative departments are rendered in two parts —

1. Entry Element Part
2. Secondary Element Part

Entry Element Part

Entry element part or portion of Administrative Department, denotes the subject and the work of the department. The portion or part which reflect the nature of working or the subject, is put as Entry Element and written in Capital letters.

Example :

Ministry of Finance, Govt. of India.

		INDIA, FINANCE (Ministry of —).

Use of Dash

If the Entry Element occurs in any position :

(a) In the beginning of the Name

(b) In the middle of the Name

(c) In the end of the Name

The position of the Entry Element Part/portion will be indicated by the Dash '—'

Example :

Government of India Ministry of Information and Broadcasting.

(a) INDIA — As Geographical Entity.

(b) INFORMATION AND BROADCASTING — the Part of the name indicating the work and subject of the department. Hence it is a Entry Element.

(c) (Ministry of —). It is rest portion of the Name of the department. Hence it is Secondary Element.

Secondary Element

The portion/part which not a Entry Element is considered as Secondary Element.

Secondary Element is rendered as under —

(a) Clubs in circular brackets.

(b) Rest or left part/portion of the department is written in circular bracket.

(c) It is written in ordinary hand.

(d) The first letter and the first letter of the proper Nouns is written in Capital letter.

(e) The sequence of the Entry Element will be indicated by '—' Dash.

		INDIA, EDUCATION (Ministry of —).

UTTAR PRADESH, EDUCATION
(District-Officer) (Lucknow).

Other of the Department

UNITED STATES OF AMERICA, EDUCATION (Bureau of—)

Entry Element
Connecting
Secondary Element
the sequence

MADHYA PRADESH, EXCISE (Department of—)

MADRAS, INSTRUCTIONS (Department of Public—).

Officer of the Department

Every Department is Headed by an officer's Post having a Designation. If an Administrative Department has no special name, the Designation of its officer is to be used as its name.

Example :

RAJASTHAN, SCHOOLS (Inspector of—)

INDIA, ARCHAEOLOGICAL (District-officer).

UP, EDUCATION (Deputy Director of—) (Agra circle).

UP, MAGISTRATE (District) (Kanpur).

Homonym in Administrative Department

MADRAS, EDUCATION (District-
Officer) (Salem).

If two or more Administrative Departments of the same Government have Similar Names, the Individualising Element for resolving the Homonym is to be an appropriate term denoting either :

1. Its area of Jurisdiction;
2. Its function; or
3. Its headquarters; or
4. Any other necessary and sufficient attribute.

Example :

KARNATAKA, EDUCATION (Deputy Director of —)

KARNATAKA, EDUCATION (Deputy Director of —) (Administration)

GUJARAT, SCHOOLS (Inspector of —) (Ahmedabad).

GUJARAT, SCHOOLS (Inspector of —) (Baroda).

Interpolation of Sub-Headings

If an Administrative Department is a organ of Second remove or Last remove and its name involves —

(a) Homonym

(b) Not individualising

and the homonyms are not removed, and cannot be removed/ resolved without the addition of the name(s) of the organ of earlier remove in its hierarchy. In such cases such names are to be interpolated as sub-heading between the name of the Government as a whole and of the Name of the Administrative Department in question.

In view of the above it is explained that if there is homonym (i) in the first order of whole of the Government (ii) in the second order which is subordinate of the first order (iii) in the third order which is subordinate to second order (iv) in the later or last order which is subordinate to its superior department of first step above, the homonym will be resolved by the Individualising Element.

Example :

1. INDIA, EDUCATION (Ministry of —) (New Delhi).
2. INDIA, EDUCATION (Ministry of —), EDUCATION (Committee)(New Delhi).

3. INDIA, EDUCATION (Department of —), EDUCATION (Directorate), EDUCATION (District-officer) (Nagpur Circle).

But a minimum number of such sub-headings should be inserted in their descending be interpolated. If the number of such headings is two or more, they should be inserted. Only such sub-heading should be interpolated which are essential and responsible for the thought contents.

Temporary Organ

If there is temporary organ or *Ad hoc* organ (Department or Subordinate Department, Committee, Unit, Center, Bureau, etc) appointed temporarily or for some specific purpose or time, such organ should be put under the whole Government or the Parent department.

Example :

INDIA, EDUCATION (Commission) (1982).

UP, EDUCATION (Department), ACCOUNT (Committee) (1971-2).

In case of a Temporary organ of a Government its year of formation is to be added as an Individualising Element.

Name of the Chairman

If it is a *Ad hoc* Commission or Committee of a Government, the Name of the Chairman is to be added within Circular brackets after the Individualising Element in the following Manner :

1. The term "Chairman",
2. A colon ':' and
3. The words in the reduced Name of the Chairman written in their Natural sequence.

Example :

Whole Govt. Parent Department, Commission, (Year) (Chairman : name of chairman).

OR

Whole Government, Commission (Year) (Chairman : name)

In other words, The de facto responsibility for the thought and expression constituting a work may rest solely on a

Temporary organ of a Government. The organ of the Government is taken to be the author of such work.

Y,741;4355:6,7'N31t N33

CHINA, FLOOD RELIEF (National Commission) (1931) (Chairman : T.V. Soong).

Report.

236

INDIA, TAXATION ENQUIRY (Commission) (1953) (Chairman : John Mathai).

Report. X72N53t

Example :

Common Organ of the Government

When two bodies or Government set up a organ or a body jointly, it is to be preceded by the name of the Government setting it up; and a common conjunction is to connect them.

Example :

UNITED STATES and CANADA, REHABILITATION (Commission).

INDIA, LOK SABHA and RAJYA SABHA, BANK BILL (Joint Commission on —) (Chairman: M.M. Joshi).

UP and RAJASTHAN, ACADEMIC (Mixed – Committee) (Chairman: P.N. Thakur).

INDIA, LOK SABHA and RAJYA SABHA, BANK BILL (Joint Commission —) (Chairman : MM Joshi).

22

INSTITUTION

An independent or autonomous corporate body other than a Government. It may be created by a Government, or constituted under the statute or formed voluntarily — either formally or unformally. It has or it is intended to have continued existence or functions beyond that of merely convening a conference.

or

An organ of an institute which is independent or Autonomous corporate body <u>other than Government</u>.

In other words any autonomous or even non-autonomous organizations, engaged in the work of research, production, commerce and supply of commodities and services to the public, may have to be taken to be the Institutional author for a work for whose thought and expression it is responsible. It is so even if the Institute is owned and managed by the Government, but function as autonomous body not controlled by Government fully.

Special Features of an Institution

1. It is not a Government body (a body other than the Government).
2. It may or may not be created by the Government.
3. It may be created by a private agency.
4. It may be created by a Group of persons, societies, trusts or other bodies.
5. It may be created formally under status of the Government or Government rules and regulations.
6. It may be created informally under or resulted discussions or decisions.

7. It may be an Autonomous body.
8. It may also be an Non-Autonomous body.
9. It may be engaged in Research and development of the society.
10. It may be of any type — Economic body, Political body, Social body, Academic body, Religious body or any other body BUT not a Government body.

Problem to Decide

There may be conflict to decide whether it is a Government body or an Institution. The conflict of Authorship may be resolved on the following analogy —

1. It depend on the ability and intelligency of the cataloguer on the basis of his experience.
2. Periodical reviews may help to resolve the conflict.
3. No doubt, there are few similar features among Government and Institutional authorship. But it may be resolved by discussing on the following points —
   (a) Whether it is not a Government control under the Government as a whole or the parent body of the Government.
   (b) Whether it is not a organ, 1, 2, 3 of any pure Government department and put under the direct control of the Government department.
   (c) It is NOT a work bearing on a discharge of primary function of Government-Administrative report of the Government, deliberative between two or more Governments, directions of the Government, any other work embodying thoughts created and expressed by the Government as a whole or by an organ of Government of any remove.
   (d) The responsibility for the thought and expression constituting a work may rest solely on an Institution. An organ of an institution may also be the author of a work.

Conflict about DELEGATION

There are two types of delegations —

1. Delegation to a conference,

2. Delegation to an international body.

Delegation is itself a corporate body.

It implies two other corporate bodies —

1. Delegated-from-body.
2. Delegated-to-body.

The kind of documents, about whose authorship conflict arises, may comprise —

(a) Memoranda submitted,

(b) Resolutions tabled,

(c) Utterances made

— by the delegation at the conference,

(d) and report by the Delegation to the Delegated-from-body.

Delegation is not an independent body but an organ. Hence name of the body of which it is an organ or the parent body of which the delegation is an organ, should be mentioned along with its own name to establish its identity.

Now the question arises whether 'Is it an organ of the Delegated-from-body or of the Delegated-to-Body'? Answer is 'which body takes the ultimate responsibility for the thought content of the document created by the delegation'? Is it the Delegated-from-body or Delegated-to-Body?

Hence, the Delegated-from-Body should be taken to be the parent body of a Delegation to a conference or to the body such as United Nations, or a peace conference in respect of any work embodying any thought and expression created by the Delegation.

However, each of the following Institutions should be taken as Author of its works, as if it were independent of the parent body, if it exists, be it institutions.

1. **Independent existence**

Bank

Board of Trades

Cathedral

Cemetery

Stock Exchange

Firms of Enterprise

Foundations

Guild

Chamber of Commerce	Masonic Body
Church	Monastery
College, University	Mosque
Convent	Temples
Endowment	Muth
	Park
	Gardens

2. **Having distinctive name**

Political party	Botanical gardens
Festival name	Museum
Hospital	Observatory
Laboratory	Shop
Library	Zoological garden
Exhibition	Other Non-Government bodies

3. If no distinctive name, it should be treated organ of its parent body.
4. If having distinctive name and is a formal and informal group of the members of a parent body for creative, or any other economical or social purpose should be treated as an organ of the parent body.
5. Any section or branch of an institution should be taken as author, as if it were independent of its parent body.

   If the section or branch has no distinctive name, it should be treated as organ of the parent body.
6. Each International Institution or conference of private persons, non-government institutions should be taken as author of work made up of its deliberations.

The following bodies are NOT considered as Institutions —

(a) Charter granted by a Government to a city or rural district or any Government department.

(b) Law of territory.

(c) Constitution of dependence

(d) Decision of court of law

(e) Report of legal proceedings

(f) Judgement of legal courts

(g) Legal proceedings

Examples :

LIBRARY (Madras-Association)

LIBRARY (Association) (Great Britain), COUNCIL.

2, 31 N31

LIBRARY (American-Association),

EDUCATION (— Committee), ELEMENTARY

(— sub-committee).

241

Examples :

Indian statutory commission's statement and recommendations/by Landholders of India/British Library Association, London, 1932. Acc. 243 Call No. 4, 44; 2N28t:g (Z, 44, 211,1) N327

V, 44;2 N28t;g 9Z,44,211,1) N32

LANDHOLDERS (— of India).

243

23

CONFERENCE

It is a Ad-hoc assembly for deliberation or formulation and expression of opinion or sentiments.

It is not convened by a Government and made up solely of its own personnel or as a Constituent Assembly to form a Sovereign state.

1. It is an Institution and made up solely of its members or as a Foundation Assembly to form an Institution, or more than one Government jointly or confined solely to their own personnel or more than one institutions jointly or confined solely to their members.
2. Conference is convened or conducted by —
   (a) a number of persons and/or corporate bodies, spontaneously, to consider matters of common interest, or
   (b) a body with no functions or existence beyond the conference convened and held by it, or
   (c) a body with only the convening or holding of conferences at intervals, as its primary function.

Example :

1. Indian Mathematical Conference of 1957.
2. The Reception Committee of Indian Mathematical Conference of 1957.

Conference as Author

The responsibility for the thought and expression constituting a work may rest solely on a conference. The conference is taken to be the author of such work. A conference may be either a non-periodical or a periodical one. The 'Proceedings' of a periodical conference is to be catalogued in accordance with periodical publications.

Example :

1. Proceedings of International Swedenborg Conference/ Held in connection with the celebrations of Swedenborg Society's Centenary/London/July 4-8, 1910 / Third edition / The Swedenborg Society/Institute/1810/ London/1912. D, 6 x k88 p1, N10 N12 Acc. 245.

D, 6 x K88p1, N10 N12
SWEDENBORG (International-
Conference) (London) (1910).
Proceedings. Ed 3.
The conference was held in connection
with the celebrations of the Swedenborg
Society's centenary.

245

2. Proceedings of the All-India conference of librarians/ Held at Lahore/4-8 Jan. 1918 / Shimla / Printed at Govt. Monotype Press / 1918. Call No. 2p4, N30 N30 Acc. 247

2p44, N18 N18
LIBRARIANS (All India Conference
of —) (Lahore) (1918).
Proceedings.

247

Rendering of Conference

The rendering of the name of a conference is to be on the analogy of Institutions. (JD).

1. The name of the conference,
2. Place of the conference,
3. Year of the conference.

Individualising Element

The name of the place of a conference and its year are to be added as Individualising Elements to the name of a conference which is not held periodically.

It is not applied for periodical conference.

Example :

GANDHI MEMORIAL MEETING (Lucknow) (1956).

INTERNATIONAL PEACE CONFERENCE (The Hague) (1899).

POLITICAL SUFFERER's CONFERENCE (Gauhati) (1933).

DIPLOMATIC CONFERENCE

These conferences are not held periodically. The name of the peace of a Diplomatic conference is to be prefixed to the name of the conference so as to form a word-group, if it is not already in the name of the conference.

The year of the conference is to be added as Individualizing Element.

Example :

GENEVA SUMMIT CONFERENCE (1956).

PARIS PEACE CONFERENCE (1919).

Conference without specific name

The conference which have —

1. no specific name
2. not held periodically

— is to be made of the name of the class of persons meeting together as conference, such as —

(a) Citizens,

(b) Indian Residents,

(c) Ladies,

(d) Merchants,

(e) Musicians,

(f) Professionals and occupants

(g) Etc. etc. of the same type.

The name of the place of meeting is to be added as Individualising Element to the name of the conference. The year, month and date of the conference is to be added as Second Individualising Element.

Example :

1. CITIZENS (Lucknow).
2. INDIAN RESIDENTS (London) (1961).
3. NON-RESIDENT INDIAN'S CONFERENCE (Delhi) (Jan., 2003).
4. ENGINEER's CONFERENCE (Patna) (1998).
5. INDIAN MERCHANTS CONFERENCE (Delhi) (1973).
6. WOMEN'S LIBERATIONS CONFERENCE (Nagpur) (2001).
7. IIARYANA MUSICIANS CONFERENCE (Chandigarh) (1976).
8. INDIAN WRITERS CONVENTION (Madras) (1987).

Conference as Organ

If the conference is a organ of another corporate body, it is to be given a multiple corporate heading.

Example :

INDIA and PAKISTAN CITIZENS' CONFERENCE (Islamabad) (June 23-26, 1982).

JOINT CONFERENCE OF INDIA and IRAQ WOMEN'S (Bagdad) (1989).

Conference with Parent Body

If a Conference is held or organized by a parent body, the Conference is to be treated as organ of the Parent Body and the Heading in which the name of the conference is rendered is to be proceeded by the Headings specifying its Parent Body which may itself be an organ.

Example :

1. MADRAS, COLLECTORS' CONFERENCE (Ootacamund) (1918).
2. LUCKNOW (UNIVERSITY), TEACHERS CONFERENCE (1987).
3. LIBRARY (Indian-Association), COLLEGE LIBRARIANS CONFERENCE (Agra) (1978).

Conference with Joint Parent Bodies

If the Parent Body of an organ conference consists jointly of two or more corporate bodies, the name of each Parent Body is to precede the name of the conference. The names of the Parent bodies are to be connected by a conjunction.

Example :

1. MADRAS, ENGINEER (Chief —) and MYSORE, ENGINEER (Chief —), PALAR RIVER CONFERENCE (Mysore) (1956).
2. The First All Asia Educational Conference/Papers offered to the/Library Service Section/Ed by SR Ranganathan/Published by The South Indian Teachers/Madras/1930.

2p 4, N30 N30

EDUCATIONAL (All Asia-Conference)
(Benaras) (1930), LIBRARY SCIENCE
(Section).

Papers offered. Ed by SR Ranganathan.

246

3. Proceedings/Rule/Seminar/of/college librarians/in/Rajasthan/Held at the/Rajasthan University Library/Jaipur/from 8-11 May, 1965/Ed. By NN Gidwani/Director of Libraries/Rajasthan University, Jaipur/June 1965.

	2,33p4437, N65	N65
		LIBRARY (Seminar of College —
	in	Rajasthan) (Jaipur) (1965).
		Proceedings. Ed by NN Gidwani.
	372	

24

Book Index Entry

[Rule. FN 75]

Book Index Entry is a entry other than the Main Entry, Class Index Entry, Cross Reference Entry and Cross Reference Index Entry. These entries are made under the headings of a Joint authors, title, subsequent authors, series etc.

Every document is also traced under the heading of Book Index Entries. Normally every document will get at least one Book Index Entry. It may get more than one entry, but selections more than half a dozen.

Book Index Entries are not made for Government and annual and other periodical reports, of an administrative nature, do not get any Book Index Entry.

"Book Index Entry is a specific Added Word Entry in a Dictionary Catalogue".

These entries enable a reader to get his document, provided he has some information or other about it. For, Book Index Entries enter a document under the name of the authors, editors, translators, etc, under the name of series and in certain cases, under the title.

Hence, Book Index Entries are important entries which can not be avoided as such entries meet the Reader's approach in various directions.

Rendering

The Book Index Entry is to consist successively of the following sections :

1. Leading section,
2. Second section,

3. Index Number,
4. Note section, if any.

One Entry of two headings [Rule. MK 01]

If two or more entries are alike in the heading and the second section and differ only in the Index Number, they may be consolidated into one entry, the different call numbers being added in succession, one below the other in one or more columns.

Leading Section

A Book Index Entry is to be given using as Heading each of such of the following as the Main Entry of the book admit of —

1. Other than class Index Entry heading. Heading, which is not used as Heading in Class Index Entry, will be used for Book Index Entry.

2. Permutation of Names in the Heading. If it is a heading of two joint authors, or two collaborators of the same kind and also the case of a joint organ or conference of two bodies, permutation of the names of the two corporate bodies in the Main Heading; and in case of personal author and a corporate author, permutation of the name of the personal author and of the corporate author.

In view of the above we can decide to use such Headings for Book Index Entry which are —

(a) Used as Heading of a Main Entry.
(b) Used as permutation in joint personal authors.
(c) Used as permutation in joint corporate body.
(d) Used as two collaborators used as heading in Main Entry of the same kind.
(e) If it is a heading also in case of joint organ or conference of two bodies.

Heading of Book Index Entry derived from Title Page

(a) Name of each collaborator.
(b) Permutation of the name of Joint collaborators of any kind mentioned in the title portion.

(c) Name of the first collaborator of any kind mentioned in the title portion.

(d) Name of the sponsor in case of a Bill or set.

(e) Title of a book, if it is fanciful, if it contains a proper noun, or if it is treated in usage as a proper noun.

(f) If it is not, as such, eligible to be used as Main Heading of a Class Index Entry of the book.

Book Entries derived from Note Section

1. Name of Independent series,
2. Name of Inter-dependent series
3. Heading of Extract note
4. Heading of alternative title.

General Rule

1. The second section of Book Index Entry depend on the nature of the heading.
2. Edition statement is to be given, preceding by a full stop.

Second Section of Book Index Entries

1. First or Single author Heading entry —

    Second Section - Title, Edition

2. Title as Heading —

    Second Section - By Surname of author.

3. Series as Heading —

    Second Section - Number of series [in between first vertical and second vertical surname of author(s)] : (colon) Title. Edition

Author Book Index Entries

Author which are given in Heading Section of the main entry are to be considered for Book Index Entry.

Rendering

On Leading Line

1. Name of the First author or Single author, if it is a Single author in Heading Section of Main Entry.

2. Name of two authors, if there are two authors in the Heading Section of Main Entry. The Sequence will be the same as given in Main Entry.
3. If there are two authors. There will be made two Author Book Index Entries —
   (a) By both authors in the same Sequence,
   (b) By both authors by Permutation (in reverse Sequence).

Second Heading

1. From Second vertical
2. Title of the book
3. Full stop
4. Index Number on the right side on the line the title section ends. If there is no sufficient space write on the second line and on right side corner.

JOHN (William) (1892).
Acoustics of buildings.
C30bNA,2 N31

JOHN (William) (1892) and DUFF
(James) (1930).
Accounting of buildings. C30bNA,2 N31

Collaborator as Heading

If there are collaborators other than the main authors of a document *i.e.* Editor, translator, compiler, reviser, illustrator etc., these are given in addition to the authors of a document and mentioned in the main entry in the body of the card. Such collaborators are to be entered as Heading for Book Index Entries on the leading line as follows :

1. The name of the collaborator, to be written as the author is rendered —
   - (a) Entry Element — Surname
   - (b) Secondary Element — Fore name in circular brackets
   - (c) Individualising element, if any (Date of birth — Date of death) in circular bracket.
   - (d) Comma
   - (e) Designation of the collaborator and underline
   - (f) Full stop
2. The surname of the main authors (from second verticals and from next line and new paragraph).
3. Colon
4. Title of the book
5. Full stop.

Index Number

Index number (Call number is called Index Number in the Book Index Entries and subject entries) :

1. It is written at the end on right hand side where the entries of Book Index Entries ends.
2. If no space on the line where entries end, write on the next line on right side corner.

FISCHER (Ferdinand) (1843), Rev.
Wagner: Chemical Technology.
F NO4

VERMA (PK) and DAY (RN), Ed.
Mohan Kumar : Chemical Technology.
FNO4

25

Title as Heading

Title will be used as Heading for Book Index Entry, if title is —

(a) Fanciful Title

(b) If it contains a proper noun,

(c) If it is treated in usage as a proper noun; provided that:

1. It has been used as Heading of the Main Entry.
2. It is not, as such, eligible to be used as the Main Heading of a Class Index Entry of the book.

If Title is suitable and considered for Book Index Entry, rendering will be as under —

1. Title as Heading on leading line from first vertical
2. Full stop
3. On the second line, from Second vertical —

(a) The word 'By'

(b) The Surname of the author(s)

(c) a full stop

(d) Index Number on right side corner.

HERMES.
By Jones. Evl'N3 N28

	SC	IENTIFIC (Van Nostrand's —
	En	cyclopedia etc.). Ed 2.
		A'Rl, N3, N47

Series as Heading

Series is considered for Book Index Entry and the name of the series is given as Heading on leading line in Capital letters.

The other description will be as under —

1. Serial number of the series — It is written on the next line where Heading of series ends.
2. Heading of the main entry (The Surname of the author). Secondary element is to be omitted.
3. Colon.
4. Title of the book as given in main entry, with initial letter in capital.
5. Full stop
6. Edition Statement
7. Full stop
8. Index Number.

	IN	TERNATIONAL POLITICS SERIES.
	25	Srivastava : Sino-Indian relations.
	Ed	2. V2;19041 N6 K2.1

Consolidation of Series Index Entries

MADRAS LIBRARY ASSOCIATION
PUBLICATION SERIES.
19 Ranganathan : Colon Classification
Ed.4. 2:51N3 qn32
23 Ranganathan : Five laws of
Library science.Ed.2. 2N57
24 Ranganathan : Classified Catalogue
Code.Ed.4. 2:55N3 qN58

Extract Index Entry

If the extract is from a book and the specification of extract work/position is put as Heading in Heading Section of a main entry. Such extract is considered for Book Index Entry with rendering details as under —

0. Start with inverted commas.
1. The Author of the Extract as Heading on the leading line, as given in main entry.
2. A full stop.
3. The short title of the book
4. Edition statement.
5. Full stop
6. The note/phase "Extract from
7. The name of the author as given in main entry.
8. Full stop
9. The Title of the book from which the extract is taken (Host document)
10. Full stop
11. Edition
12. The Vol. Number/Chapter Number etc.
13. Clubbed with inverted
14. Full stop

Extract Index Entry

RANGANATHAN (SR).
Model Public Library Act.
(Madras Library Association, Legislative
Series. 1). 2.2.44; (z'q) N31
"Extract from
South Indian teacher, (South India
Teachers' Union). 3; 1930; 548-556".
T'm 44, N2 N30"

108

Extraction Book Index Entry

If an Extraction Note is considered for Main Entry Heading in the main Entry, a Book Index Entry is to be prepared and The author of the Host document is to be written on the leading line similar to other Author Index Entries.

Rendering will be as under —

1. Author of the Host document from which Extract is taken in the same manner as given in Heading Section of the main entry.
2. Title of the Host document as given in main entry, but from the new paragraph and Second vertical line.
3. Full stop
4. Edition Statement, after the title Statement
5. Full stop
6. Extraction Note "For Extract see from the new paragraph and second vertical line.
7. The author of the extract in full as given in Main Entry.
8. Full stop
9. The title of the Extract, as given in Main Entry. It will start from new paragraph and from second vertical.
10. Full stop
11. Index number

	RANGANATHAN (SR).	
		Five laws of Library Science. Ed.2.
		(Ranganathan series in library
	Science.12).	
		"For extract see
		Ranganathan (SR).
		Library Science and Scientific
	Methods. 29R17 N57".	
	107	

Change of Title Note (Book Index Entry)

If the main entry is made for a book/Document which has been published with its change title also in other region or country, and a note of change title is also mention in Note Section. Such books may be considered for Book Index Entry with the Heading and details as given in Heading Section of the main entry. It is also called "Author Index Entry with change-of-title".

The rendering for Book Index Entry of such documents will be given as under —

1. Name of the author of the original document as given in Heading Section of the main entry and will be written on leading line from first vertical in the same manner as given in Heading Section.
2. Title of the original document from the new paragraph and from second vertical in the same manner as given in the main entry.
3. Index Number
4. The Note "Published in U.S.A. as from the new paragraph and from first vertical in the same manner given in Main Entry. It will start within the inverted comma to be begun.
5. The change Name of the document from the new paragraph and from the second vertical in the same manner as given in the Main Entry.

6. Inverted Comma's closed
7. A Full stop.

	RUSSEL (Bertrand).	
		Education and the social order.
		"Published in USA as
		Education and the modern world". TgY N32

26

Ordinary Composite Book

A book with two or more contributions exposition and often, though not necessary, by different authors is a composite book.

A composite book provided with a single generic title to denote all the contributors collectively, is an ordinary composite book.

An ordinary composite book, except for an encyclopedia and a memorial volume, an encyclopedia and a memorial volume, is to be dealt with as a Simple Book ignoring (the names of contributors) the ordinary composite book, except for an encyclopedia and a memorial volume, an encyclopedia and a memorial volume, is to be dealt with as a Simple Book ignoring (the names of contributors) the constituent part except for the Analytical entries. If the composite book has been analyzed in any published bibliography, the Analytical entries are not be written for it.

In other words an ordinary composite book is to be dealt with a simple book ignoring the names of the contributions of the constituents except part of Index Entry.

1. If the title page gives the name of the authors and the contributors, but does not mention the contributing titles, the main entry Heading will be of the author/ collaborators. Heading will be of the author/ collaborators. There will be a mention of the name of the contribution in the absence of the contributing title and volumes, parts and chapters etc.

Example I

Musing child / editor: / R.K. Srivastava / contributors / Dr. R.S. Sinha / Dr. Ravi Sabbarwal / Dr. Harish Raijada.

Call No. L9C: 75 N35 ACC. 4319

	L9C: 75 N35	
		SRIVASTAVA (RK), Ed.
		Musing child.
	4319	

2. A document's title page consist of the author, collaborator and the name of the contributors only. But there is no detail of contributor's title or volumes, parts or chapters.

Example II

— Psychological aspects in speech / By Ramesh Dogra / Tr. By Murli Saxena contributors:

JNDube/P.N.Wahi/MukeshchandSirohi

Call No. S: 682 N51 ACC. 3120

	S : 682 N51	
		DOGRA (Ramesh).
		Psychological aspects of speech.
	Tr	by Murli Saxena.
	3120	

3. If the title page gives the name of the author and the contributors and the title, which are contributed by the

contributors along with their parts, chapters etc. It is a single book.

Rendering will be —

1. Main entry under the main author or collaborators responsible for the thought contents of the Host document or the book of common title.
2. If there are other collaborators dealt as main author or function as author, are considered to be written in the body of the card under collaborator's statements.
3. There will be Analytical Entries under each Contributor and its title as Book Index Entries.
4. There will be Cross Reference Entries from Class Number to Class Number in two ways —
   (a) Special Cross Reference Entries — 'See' entries
   (b) Chain Cross Reference Entries — 'See also' entries.

Example III

Applied physics edited by Ramanand and R.N. Singh / contributors: P.N. Das — Heading conduction. Part I; Mohan Lal — Electric elements Part II; / Dr. R.C. Sharma — Research Velocity Tr. By R.K. Sharma; Part 3. / Physical studies No. 11/ p. 221/ Mcmillan, Delhi, 1993. Acc No. 239.

Class Number - C1, N93

Part No. 1 - C4: 24

Part No. 2 - C6: 8

Part No. 3 - C3: 21

Special Cross Reference Entry

(SCRI) has following Sections —

1. Leading Section — Class Number of the contribution cross referred.
2. Its Heading omitting individualising Elements.
3. Its short title;
4. The Directing element 'See'
5. Call Number of the Host Book,
6. Heading of the Host book omitting individualising element; and

7. Title of the Host book, a full stop, specification of the place of occurrence of the Referred-from document in the form of 'P', or 'Chap', or 'Part' or 'Vol.' or any other appropriate form, followed by the number concerned.

MAIN ENTRY

C1, N31. N9
RAMANAND and SINGH (RN), Ed.
Applied Physics.

237

Special Cross Reference Entry — Part 1

C4:24
Das.
Heating conduction.
See
C1, N93 N9
Ramanand and Singh, Ed.
Applied Physics. Pt 1.

Special Cross Reference Entry — Part 2

	C6:8
	Mohan Lal.
	Electric Elements.
	See
	C1, N93
	Ramanand and Singh, Ed.
	Applied Physics. Pt 2.

Special Cross Reference Entry — Part 3

	C 6:21
	Sharma. Tr by RK Sharma
	Research Velocity.
	See
	C1, N93 N9
	Ramanand and Singh,
	Applied Physics. Pt 2.

Chain Cross Reference Entry

This entry is made for convenience. It will consist of —

1. The Document Reference-from, may be called the Document of Remove 2; and
2. The contribution in the Host Book containing the Document of remove 2, may be called document of Remove 1.

A Chain Cross Reference Entry is to consist successively of the following sections :

1. Leading Section, consisting of the Class Number of the Document of Remove 2;
2. The directing Element 'See also';
3. Heading of the document of Remove 1;
4. Title of the Document of Remove 1, a full stop, specification of the place of occurrence of the Document of Remove 2 within the document of Remove 1 in the form of 'P' or 'Chap', or 'Part', or in any other appropriate form, a comma, followed by the number concerned;
5. The description term 'Forming' followed by the specification of the place of occurrence of the Document of Remove 1 in the Host Book in the form of 'CP', or 'Chap', or 'Part', or in any other appropriate form, the Number concerned, and the term "of";
6. Call Number of the Host Book; and
7. Heading of the Host Book omitting individualising element, and its Short Title.

Chain Cross Reference Entry

	C4:2
	See also
	Das (PN).
	Heating conduction, Sec. 6.
	"Forming pt. 1 of
	C1, N93 N9
	Ramanand and Singh, Ed.
	Applied Physics".

Class Index Entry

An ordinary Composite book is to be given Class Index Entries deriving by Chain-procedure and sought Heading are to be rendered.

It is further stated that the Class Index Entries, arising out of the Class number of each of the contributions, are also to be given.

		Class Index Entries
C1	Applied Physics	
C	Physics	Fundamentals, Physics
C1	Fundamentals, Physics	Physics

Contributors Class Index Entries

C4: 24	Heating conduction
C	Physics [s]
C4	Heat, Physics [s]
C4: 2	Transference, Heat, Physics [US]
C4: 24	Conduction of Heat, Physics [s]

Class Index Entries

Conduction of Heat, Physics
Heat, Physics
Physics

C6: 8	Electric Elements
C	Physics [s]
C6	Electricity [s]
C6:	[False link]
C6: 8	Element (Nature), Electricity, Physics [s]

Class Index Entries

Element, Electricity
Electricity, Physics
Physics

C: 3 21	Research velocity
C	Physics
C3	Sound, Physics [s]
C3: 2	Propagation, Sound, Physics [US]
C3: 21	Velocity, Sound, Physics [s]

Class Index Entries

Velocity, Sound, Physics
Sound, Physics
Physics

Book Index Entries

An ordinary Composite Book is to be given Book Index Entries.

Contribution Index Entry

An ordinary Composite Book, other than Encyclopedia and memorial Volumes, is to be given Book Index Entries for each of the contributions contained in it.

Such entries are called Contribution Index Entry. These are of two types —

1. Contributor Index Entry
2. Collaborator Index Entry.

Contributor Index Entry

Contributor Index Entry consist of —

1. Leading Section - Heading of the Contribution
2. Title Section - As per rule
3. Descriptive term Such as "Forming part of ";
4. Heading of the Host Book — only Surname is written
5. A full stop
6. Its short title,
7. A full stop
8. Index Number.

DAS (PN).
Heating Conduction.
"Forming part of
Ramanand and Singh. Applied Physics".
C1, N93 N9

MOHAN LAL.
Electric Elements.
"Forming part of
Ramanand and Singh. Applied Physics".
C1, N93 N9

SHARMA (RC).
Research Velocity. Tr by RK Sharma.
"Forming part of
Ramanand and Singh. Applied Physics".
C1, N93 N9

Collaborator to Contributor Index Entry

A Collaborator To Contributor Index Entry of an ordinary Composite book is to consist successively of the following sections :

1. Leading Section
2. Second Section
3. Descriptive term such as "Forming part of —";
4. Heading of the Host Book,
5. A full stop
6. Its short title,
7. A full stop
8. Index Number.

Rendering

1. Leading Section — The leading section is to consist of the Heading made of the name(s) of the collaborator(s) of the contribution.
2. The title section is to be that of contribution
3. Heading of the host book
4. Index Number

Note = This type is called an Author Analytical. Composite books calling for them are becoming common. Author Analytical are beyond doubt of help to readers and to the Reference staff.

Collaborator-To-Contributor Index Entry

SHARMA (RK).
Research Velocity.
"Forming part of
Ramanand and Singh. Applied Physics. Pt. 3".
C1, N93 N9

FESTSCHRIFT INDEX ENTRY

Festschrift means a collection of articles published in honour of a scholar.

A Festschrift is to be given a Book Index Entry consisting the following Section :

1. Leading Section - The term "Festschrift".
2. Second Section - Name of the Person or Institute or any other entity felicitated.
3. Index Number.

Festschrift.
University of Saint Andrews.
Ap77N11

Dedicatee Index Entry

Dedicatee means the person/Body who dedicates and sponsor festschrift.

A book Index Entry is prepared in the name of Dedicatee.

1. Leading Section - Name of dedicatee
2. Second Section - Term 'Festschrift'
3. Index Number.

Dedicatee Index Entry

UNIVERSITY OF ST. ANDREWS, Ded.
Festschrist.
Ap77N11

27

Multi-Volumed Book

Multi-volumed Book means the book which contains more than one volume.

There are two types of Multi-volumed Books —

1. The type in which the constituent volumes do not have any difference in the other factors that are capable of contributing to the little portion of a Main Entry.
2. Others which may have its separate title, Year and other description. But it has no contributors.

I. Multi-volumed Book having no Special title

Such books are treated like a simple book with following rules —

1. Complete Set

If all Volumes of a book has been published —

(a) Number representing the number of volumes constituting the book,

(b) Term "V"

(c) Mention is made after edition

Example : Ed 2. 2V.

2. Uncomplete Volume

If all the volumes of a book have not been published —

(a) The Term "V", and

(b) Number of volumes published so far.

(c) A dash

(d) Space left after dash — as entries is said to be open.

(e) The Number of volumes will be written in pencil.

(f) When the new volume is received, the old number will be replaced by new volume number.

Example : V14 —

3. Incomplete Set

If all the volumes of a book, which have been published, are not possessed by the library a further sentence is to be added to the title Section, in square brackets.

(a) Term "V"

(b) Number representing the volumes 'V3' not in the library; and

(c) Term "not in library"

Example : Ed 2. [V3 not in library]

Volume Number in Cross Reference Entry

In the cross reference Entries the volume Number is to be added whenever necessary.

Book Index Entry

In the Book Index Entries, the additional sentence prescribed in 'Uncompleted set' rules is to be reported with the short title used in such entries.

Examples : Political work of / Edmund Spenser / Edited by J.P. Collier / in five volumes / London / George Bell and some /1891.Half Title page – The Aldine Edition / of British poets. No.5. 0,111,1J52XN91.1 to, M91.5.

0,111,1J52 x M91.1 6M91.5
SPENSER (Edmund).
Poetical works. Ed by J Payne
Collier. 5v.
(Adine edition of the British
Poets. 5).

276-280

V44; 2, N28t N30.1 t N30.2
GREAT BRITAIN, INDIAN
(— Statutory Commission) (1928)
(Chairman : John Simon).
Report. 2V.
V1. Survey
V2. Recommendations.

0,111,3L71w N32.1-N32.2N32.4
SCOTT (Walter) (1771).
Letters. Ed. By HJC Grierson.
V4- [V3 not in library].
V1. 1787 – 1807
V2. 1808 – 1911
V4. 1814 – 7

73352-4

UK 44, N58 K 8.2 -
Gazetteer of India. 2V.
V1. Country and People.
V2. Indian Economy.

63471-2

Example : His Royal Highness the Duke of Edinburgh study conference on the human problems of Industrial communities written the Commonwealth and Empire. 9-27 July 1956 / Volume 1 / Report and Proceeding / 1956/London/Oxford University Press /New York V.2 Background Papers and Index.

Call No. X: 97 p1 - 2N56 J6.1 - J6.2

Accession No. 32564 – 5

X:97P1-3,n56 J6.1-J6.2
STUDY CONFERENCE ON THE
HUMAN PROBLEMS....... (Commonwealth
and Empire) (Oxford) (1956).
Proceedings and papers, 2V.
V1. Report and Proceedings.
V2. Background Papers and Index.

32563-5

CLASS INDEX ENTRIES

INDUSTRIAL RELATION ECONOMICS.
For document in this Class and its Subdivisions
see the Classified Part of the catalogue under the
Class Number X : 97

ECONOMICS
For document in this Class and its Subdivisions
see the Classified Part of the catalogue under the
Class Number X

BOOK INDEX ENTRY

STUDY CONFERENCE ON THE
HUMAN PROBLEMS OF INDUSTRIAL
COMMUNITIES WITHIN THE
COMMONWEALTH AND EMPIRE
(Oxford) (1956).
Proceedings and Papers. 2V.
X:97p1-3, N56 J 6.1-J6.2

Industrial relation.
Economics.
Economics.
Study conference on the human problems of industrial communities within the Commonwealth and Empire (Oxford) (1956).

II. Multi-Volume Book having special title other than the common title

Rending will be as follows —

1. The Term "V"
2. The Number of the Volume
3. A full stop
4. The special title of the volume
5. The term "by" followed by the name of the distinctive collaborator(s), if any;
6. A full stop
7. A Note in Circular brackets, if necessary, to indicate any other special features.

Additional Paragraph

In such book an additional paragraph is given and to be added in the Title Section of the main entry.

One Paragraph is to correspond with each volume has extra Specific information in its title page.

Numbering of Volumes

If the numbering of the volume is not normal, the corresponding portions of the paragraph are to follow what is given in the book.

Common Special Title

If two or more but not all the volumes of a set, have a common special title, they are to be given only a single paragraph in common, in the additional section of the main entry, the number of all such volume being written after the term "V" or its equivalent.

Book Index Entry

Book Index Entries of the book includes all such additional entries —

1. Which are relevant to the Special Title Section of different Volumes.
2. Additional entries will be based on Main Entry.

Call Number

The Call Number will be of —

(a) Common Class Number

(b) Followed by their Successive Book Numbers.

(c) If publication is in progress, the last Book Number is to be followed by a dash.

Book Number in Cross Reference Entry

The Book Number will be given in the corresponding note of volumes in the last after the special title connected by comma.

V1. Introduction and water to silver, N1-31.

V2. Aluminium to xenon, N5658.

MAIN ENTRY

T:(X) K7.1-K7.2)
TEACHERS (National) Council of—)
(New Delhi).
Education and Economics. 2V.
V1. Statistics in Education. Ed by
R.K. Singh.
V2. Economic Application in
Education.

523-4

TRACING

Economics, Education
Education.
Teachers (National
Council of—) (New Delhi).
Education and Economics.
Singh (R.K.), Ed.
Statistics in Education
Economics Application in
Education.

ECONOMIC, EDUCATION.
For document in this Class and its Subdivisions
see the Classified Part of the catalogue under the
Class Number C1, N93 N9

One more Class Index Entry under EDUCATION

TEACHERS (National Council of —)
New Delhi.
Education and Economics. 2V.
T: (x) K7.1-K7.2

EDUCATION and ECONOMICS.
By Teachers (National Council
of —). T : (x) K7.1-K7.2

SINGH (RK), <u>Ed.</u>
Teachers (National Council of—):
Education and Economics. V1.
T : (x) K7.1

STATISTICS IN Education.
By TEACHERS (National Council
of —). V1. T : (x) K7.1

ECONOMIC APPLICATION in Education.

By TEACHERS (National Council of —). V2.

T : (x) K7.2

28

Artificial Composite Book

It is of two types :

1. Ordinary composite book,
2. Artificial composite book

ORDINARY COMPOSITE BOOK

A book of two or more contributions, each with its own title, not forming a continuous exposition and often, though not necessarily, by different authors is a composite book. A composite book is provided with a single generic title to denote all the contributions collectively, is an ordinary composite book.

An ordinary composite book, except for an Encyclopedia and memorial volume, is to be dealt with as a simple book ignoring (the names of contributors) the constituent parts except for the analytic entries — that is Cross Reference Entries and Contributor Index Entries.

If the composite book has been analysed in any published bibliography, the Analytical Entries are not to be written for it.

Example :

Italian short stories/Edited by R. Trevelyam/1964
Call Number 0121, 3xNo9K4
Acc. No. 2393

Contents

1. Removal/By Vasco Pratolini/Tr. By Swinglehurst p. 11-29 Class No. 0121, 3M21,1.
2. Houses/By Cesare Pavese/p. 30-49 Class No. 0121, 3N02,1
3. The Poor/By C. Camalo/Tr. By Authony Rhodea. P. 50-69 Class No. 0121, 3N02,1

0121, 3xN09 K4

TREVELYAM (R) Ed.

Italian Short stories.

2393

Cross Reference Entry (Special)

0121, 3M21, 1

Pratolini.

Removal.

See

0121, 3x N09 K4

Travelyam, Ed.

Italian Short stories. P. 11-29.

0121, 3N09, 1

Pavese.

House.

See

0121, 3xN09 K4

Trevelyam, Ed.

Italian short stories. P. 30-49.

0121, 3N02, 1
Camalo.
Poor.
<u>See</u>
0121, 3xN09 K4
Trevelyam, <u>Ed.</u>
Italian short stories. P.50-69.

Cross Index Entries

FICTION, ITALIAN.
For document in this Class and its Subdivisions, see the Classified Part of the catalogue under the Class Number 0121, 3

ITALIAN LITERATURE.
For document in this Class and its Subdivisions. see the Classified Part of the catalogue under the Class Number 0121

REMOVAL, PRATOLINI (Vasco) (1821)
FICTION, ITALIAN.
For document in this Class and its Subdivisions, see the Classified Part of the catalogue under the Class Number 0121, 3M21, 1

PRATOLINI (Vasco) (1821), FICTION, ITALIAN.
For document in this Class and its Subdivisions, see the Classified Part of the catalogue under the Class Number 0121, 3M21

HOUSES, PAVESE (Cesare) (1909),
FICTION, ITALIAN.
For document in this Class and its Subdivisions, see the Classified Part of the catalogue under the Class Number 0121, 3N09, 1

PAVESE (Cesare) (1909),
FICTION, ITALIAN.
For document in this Class and its Subdivisions, see the Classified Part of the catalogue under the Class Number 0121, 3N09

POOR, CAMALO (Carlo) (1902),
FICTION, ITALIAN.
For document in this Class and its Subdivisions,
see the Classified Part of the catalogue under the
Class Number 0121, 3NO2, 1

CAMALO (Carlo) (1902),
FICTION, ITALIAN.
For document in this Class and its Subdivisions,
see the Classified Part of the catalogue under the
Class Number 0121, 3NO2

TREVELYAM (R), Ed.
Italian short stories.
0121, 3xNO9 K4

SWINGLEHORST (Pamela), Tr.
Pratoline : Removal.
"Forming part of
Trevelyam, Ed: Italian short stories".
0121, 3xNO9 K4.

PAVESE (Cesare) (1909).
Houses.
"Forming part of
Trevelyam, Ed: Italian short stories".
0121, 3xNO9 K4

RHODEA (Authony), Tr.
Camalo : Poor.
"Forming part of
Trevelyam, Ed: Italian short stories".
0121, 3xNO9 K4

SWINGLEHURST (Pamela), Tr.
Pratoline : Removal.
"Forming part of
Trevelyam, Ed: Italian short stories".
0121, 3xNO9 K4

TRACING

0121, 3M21	p. 11-19	Fiction Italian.
0121, 3NO9	p. 30-49	Italian Literature.
0121, 3NO9	p. 50-59	Removal, Pratolini (vasco) (1821), Fiction, Italian.
		Pratolini (Vasco) (1821), Fiction, Italian.
		House, Pavese (Cesare) (1909), Fiction, Italian.

Pavese (Cesare) (1909),
Fiction Italian.
Poor Camalo (Carlo) (1902),
Fiction Italian.
Camalo (Carlo) (1902),
Fiction Italian.
Pavese, Houses
Trevelyam (R), Ed.
Swinglehurst (Pamela), Tr.
Rhodea (Authony), Tr.

The following additional entries will be made in case of ordinary composite book in addition to Main Entry —

1. Cross Reference Entries —
   (a) Special Cross Reference Entries,
   (b) Chain Cross Reference Entries
2. Class Index Entries
3. Cross Reference Index Entries
4. Book Index Entries
5. Contribution Index Entries
6. Contributor Index Entry
7. Tracing

1. Cross Reference Entries

The Cross Reference Entries of an ordinary composite books are to be of two types :

(a) Special; and

(b) Chain

(a) Special Cross Reference Entries. It consists of —

(i) Leading Section — Class Number of contribution cross referred.

(ii) Its heading omitting individualising elements.

(iii) The Directing Element "see"

(iv) Call Number of the Host Book

(v) Heading of the Host Book omitting individualising element.

(vi) Title of the Host Book, a full stop, specification of occurrence of the referred from document in the form of "P" or "Chap", or "Part", or in any other appropriate form followed by the Number concerned.

	2:97 (x:9)y.7
	Kaula.
	Documentation in Social Science.
	See
	2:97 N63
	Ranganathan, Ed.
	Documentation and its facets.
	Chap. F6.

(b) Chain Cross Reference Entries. This entry is for convenience:

1. Document Referred-from
2. Contribution in the Host Book

Chain Cross Reference Entry consists of —

(a) Leading Section — Class Number of contribution

(b) The Directing Element "see also"

(c) Heading of the Document (contribution)

(d) Title of the contribution, a full stop

(e) Specification of place (location)

(f) Term "Forming" followed by specification of the place of occurrence and the term 'of'

(g) Call Number of the Host Book

(h) Heading of the Host book omitting individualising element, a full stop, and its short title.

2:519 (x:93)
See also
Kaula (PN).
Documentation in Social Science, Sec. 9.
"Forming Chap. F6 of
2:97 N63
Ranganathan, Ed.
Documentation and its facets".

3. Book Index Entry —
   (a) Contributor Index Entry
   (b) Collaborator Index Entry
4. Class Index Entry
5. Cross Reference Index Entry.

ARTIFICIAL COMPOSITE BOOK

Main Entry

In the Artificial Composite Book, the main entry is to be constructed as if it were the main entry of the first constituent work except that to this is to be added a section for each later constituent work. Further, the descriptive term "Composite Book" is to be added after the Call Number at the end of the leading section.

2 :44 Composite Book

Sections

For second constituent work —

1. The Number "2"
2. Heading appropriate to it.

3. A colon
4. Its title proper with the initial letter in capital
5. A full stop
6. Notes, if any, and
7. Its Call Number, written at the right end of the last line of the section.
8. Various parts of the section.
9. The paragraph giving the entry for any other constituent work is to be similar to the entry for the second constituent work, except that the appropriate serial number is to take the place of "2".

NOTE

If all the constituent works belong to the same series, a note need not to be written in the section of each constituent work. It is sufficient if a single note is added as the final section, the serial number part of the section consisting of the successive serial numbers.

MAIN ENTRY

C633:23 N11

HENDERSON (Archibold) (1877).
Twenty-seven lines upon the cubic
Surface.
2 Wood (P W) : Twisted cubic with the
Cubical hyperbola.
B6363:23 N13
(Cambridge tracts in Mathematics and
Mathematical physics. 13, 14).

Additional Entries other than Main Entry

1. Cross Reference Entry —
   (a) Special Cross Reference Entry
   (b) Ordinary Cross Reference Entry

2. Class Index Entry
3. Cross Reference Index Entry
4. Book Index Entry
5. Tracing

1. Special Cross Reference Entry

A Special Cross Reference entry is to be given from the Call Number of each of the second and the succeeding constituent works.

It consists of —

(a) Leading section — Call number of constituent work cross referred.

(b) Its heading

(c) Its title

(d) The descriptive term "Bound as part 2 with" or "Permitted as part—with" as the case may be.

(e) Call Number of the Leading section of Main Entry

(f) Heading of main entry

(g) Colon

(h) Short title of first constituent work.

(i) A full stop.

B6363 : 23 N13
Wood (PW).
Twisted cubic with the cubical
Hyperbola.
<u>Bound as part 2 with</u>
B6363 : 23 N11
Henderson : Twenty-seven lines upon
the cubic surface.

2. Ordinary Cross Reference Entry

A ordinary cross reference entry is to be given from every topic in each of the constituent works, which may call for it :

(a) Call Number, the heading and the short title are to be those of the first constituent work.

(b) The part and the pages of reference, if any, are to be given.

(c) The descriptive term "composite book" is to be added after the call number.

3. Class Index Entry.

4. Cross Reference Index Entry — Appropriate to each constituent work.

5. Book Index Entry —

Appropriate to each constituent work —

(a) Descriptive term "Bound as part 2 with" or "Printed as part 2 with".

(b) Index Number of the first constituent work.

WOOD (PW).
Twisted Cubic.
Bound as part 2 with
B6363 : 23 N11
Handerson : Twenty-seven lines upon
the cubic surface.

29

Periodical Publication

It is one of the kind of periodical publications which is —

1. A volume, or a small group of volumes of it, is intended to be published or completed normally once in a year/ or at other regular intervals, though irregularity in interval is not ruled out.
2. Each successive volume, or periodical group of volumes, is usually distinguished by the year of publication and/or by a number belonging to a system of simple or complex ordinal number. Such number is usually called VOLUME NUMBER.
3. Periodical publication is always published with the intention of continuous publication.
4. Periodical may be —
   (a) Continued permanently,
   (b) Ceased its publications,
   (c) Irregular in publication,
   (d) Split in to more than one publications,
   (e) Amalgamated with other periodical.
5. Periodical publication may have —
   (a) Single-worded name,
   (b) Multi-worded name,
   (c) Complex name,
   (d) Subordinate or additional name,
   (e) Name changed.
6. A periodical may be published by an —
   (a) Agency,

(b) Publisher,

(c) Individual,

(d) Corporate body,

(e) Government.

7. A periodical publication may have different periodicity—

(a) Annual,

(b) Half-yearly,

(c) Quarterly,

(d) Monthly,

(e) Fortnightly,

(f) Weekly,

(g) Bi-Annual,

(h) Etc.

8. A periodical publication may have —

(a) One volume to be completed in one year,

(b) One volume to be completed in two years,

(c) One volume to be completed in six months.

9. Periodical publication may have —

(a) Each volume made up of distinct and independent contributions,

(b) Not confirming a continuous exposition,

(c) Normally by two or more personal authors,

(d) Normally the specific subjects,

(e) The authors of the contributions in successive volumes being (generally) different,

(f) All the subjects falling within one and the same region of knowledge, contemplated to be brought within its purview,

(g) It is not usually released complete as a volume but only a fascicules or numbers, as they are called,

(h) It essentially expound knowledge and not repeat the same kind of information,

(i) Usually in the same pattern,

(j) In each of its volumes just bringing the information up to date from volume to volume,

(k) It is also used to denote any single volume of a periodical.

Example :

1. Annals of Library Science
2. Library and Librarian
3. Proceedings of Royal Society of London
4. Chemical Abstract

Complexities

Periodical publications form of the sources of perplexity in cataloguing practice. Their vagaries may transcend all imagination and anticipation.

Periodical publications include the detail of sponsor, name, periodicity, format, pagination, excrescential attachment to all or stray volumes.

There involves many complexities —

1. Irregularity in Volume-Number

(a) Change in volume-periodicity.

(b) Volume being numbered in two or more sequences, the sequences being termed new series, first series, second series etc. or by similar names.

(c) Volumes being numbered simultaneously in two or more sequences.

2. Irregularity in Publication

(a) Non-publication of volumes in certain periods, but the sequence of volume numbers being continuous.

(b) Break in the sequence or irregularity in the numbering of volumes due to non-publication or other causes.

(c) Two or more volumes published as a single volume or bound as a single volume.

3. Change of Title and Sponsor

(a) Change of title, or of sponsor, or of both, but the numbering of the volumes being continued in the original sequence.

(b) Change of title, or of sponsor or of both with change in the sequence of volume numbers.

4. Amalgamation. (Joining of two organization to form one other organization)

(a) One periodical publication amalgamated in other periodical publication and numbering of volumes continued in its original sequence.

(b) One periodical publication amalgamated in other periodical publication but numbering of volumes are changed in the sequence of volume numbers.

(c) Two periodical publications amalgamated under a new title with its class number the same as that of one of the publications amalgamated.

(d) Amalgamation of two or more publications under a new title and with its class number different from that of any of them.

5. Splitting. (Dividing)

(a) Splitting up into two or more periodical publications with one of them, having the original class number.

(b) Splitting up into two or more periodical publications, the original class number not being borne by any of them.

(c) A periodical with many independent or dependent issues contains two or more periodicals, with or without a generic title, but has to be split into independent periodicals, either associated or not, on the completion of a volume.

6. Supplement

(a) A periodical publication may have Monograph 'Supplement' or Book 'Supplement' without separate pagination and title page. These may have separate pagination and title page.

(b) The supplement having a sequence but having separate pagination and title page and each supplement being regarded as a periodical publication by itself.

(c) The supplement may be a cumulative index of main publication periodical.

Irregularity at a glance

Irregularity in Volume Number

Irregularity - (a) Change in periodicity
(b) Different sequence
(c) Simultaneous numbering in two or more sequences.

Irregularity in Publication

(a) No publication in certain period but numbering of volumes continuous.
(b) Break in sequence but numbering of volumes irregular.
Vol. 23; 1981 — Vol. 24; 1983
(c) Publication of two or more volumes in single volume.
Exp.: Vol. 2-3; 1980-81

Change in Title and Sponsor

(a) Change in title Change in sponsor Change in both Title and sponsor	But numbering of Volumes is continuous as was in original
(b) Change in title Change in sponsor Change in both Title and sponsor	But change in Numbering of volumes with the change in title, sponsor or both.

Amalgamation

(a) Two or more periodicals amalgamated =	But the name of any one is continued but numbering continued as in original
(b) Two or more periodicals amalgamated =	But the name of any one is continued with change in Numbering of volumes
(c) Two or more periodicals amalgamated =	But under new title with same class number
(d) Two or more periodicals amalgamated =	But under new title with different class number other than the originals.

Splitting (Divided)

(a) If one periodical is separated or divided in two or more periodical	=	But having the original class number
(b) If one periodical is separated or divided in two or more periodical	=	But both having different class number than the original
(c) Multiple periodical (Periodical having separate parts, sections, units)	=	(i) Contains issue of two or more periodicals (ii) With or without generic title (iii) Or split into independent periodicals (iv) Either associated or not, on the completion of volumes.

Supplement (A thing or publication which is added to something else to improve or complete it)

(a) Supplement with continuous pagination and title page.

(b) Supplement with separate pagination and title page.

(c) More supplements or extra volumes having separate pagination and title page and regarded independent.

Example : Cumulative Index.

SIMPLE PERIODICAL PUBLICATION

Main Entry

It consists of —

1. Leading Section
2. Heading Section
3. Periodicity
4. Series Note
5. Holding Section
6. Tracing

1. Leading Section (Class Number)

It consists only class number [not call number], because the entry of a periodical stands for all volumes (not for one volume) to be added from time to time.

2. Heading Section. It consists of —

(a) Its title proper (Name of the periodical)

(b) Name of sponsor is omitted, if occurring in continuation of its title proper.

(c) Comma

(d) The name of its sponsor, if any.

Name of Sponsor

1. If name of sponsor occur in continuation of title proper, it should be put separately.
2. If the name of sponsor does not occur in continuation of title proper, it should be put within circular brackets.
3. The name of the sponsor is to be written in the chosen, or formally selected manner.

Title Proper

1. Title proper should be considered as heading in heading section.
2. The first two words of the title proper are to be written in Block letters.

Individualising Element

If the title proper is taken along with the sponsor, but does not individualise it, a individualising element is to be added.

(a) It is to be the name of its country, state, province, district, country, taluk, city or town. The preference should be given to greater extension.

Example :

1. Educational Review (India)
2. Educational Review (Great Britain)

Conference Proceedings

If the periodical publication consists of the proceedings of the conference held periodically, the place and the year of the conference is to be omitted.

Periodical publication as proceedings (of a conference) published periodically (published continuously after a certain period).

Section of Periodicity

Periodicity section consists of —

1. Statement of Periodicity

(A) <u>If the period is one year or less</u>, the periodicity consists of —

(a) Number of volume per year

(b) A semi-colon

(c) Number of separately bound parts in a volume, if more than one

(d) Term "parts per volume"

(e) A full stop.

(B) <u>If the period is greater than one year</u>, periodicity statement is to consist of —

(a) Term "IV for"

(b) Number indicating the number of year

(c) Term "Years"

(d) A semi-colon

(e) Number of separately bound parts in a volume, if more than one.

(f) Term "parts per volume"

(g) A full stop

(C) If the periodical publication is irregular, the statement of periodicity is to be begin with the term "Irregular".

2. Periodicity statement, after the statement of A, B, C (above), consists of —

(a) A dash

(b) Some space and a semi-colon

(c) A dash

(d) The periodicity section is to be enclosed in square brackets.

2m 44,N62
HERALD OF Library Science,
(Sarda Ranganathan Endowment
for Library Science).
[IV per year. V1 - ; 1962 -].

Em 42, N28
BULLETIN, Chemical Society of
Japan.
[Irregular. IV per year. V1 - ; 1928 -].

3. If the periodical publication continuous to be published whether taken in the library or not, no figure is to be added after the dashes within the square brackets.

No figure is added if the publication of periodical continued, whether received in the library or not.

[IV per year. VI – ; 1928 –]

Such entry is said to be "open for the publication"

4. If the publication has ceased to be published —

(a) Number of volume of the last issue

AND

(b) Year of the last volume

— are to be inserted after the respective dashes within the square brackets.

such entry is said to be "closed for the publication".

NOTE

1. Periodicity section is clubbed in square brackets because all such informations are taken from outside.
2. It is difficult to get the year of the starting the periodical, but it should be traced as gives an important bibliographical information to the readers.

SERIES NOTE

The series note is to be enclosed in square brackets. It consist of —

(a) Series

(b) Serial Number of all the volumes of the periodical publication at the end of the note.

(c) If no serial number of series is available, give the year number.

Holding Section

If the library have a continuing set of volumes of periodical, the holding section is to consists of —

1. Term "this library has"
2. Term "V"
3. The number of the earlier volume available in the library.
4. A dash
5. The number of latest volume
6. A semi-colon
7. The year of the earlier volumes available in the library
8. A dash
9. Year of the latest volume available in the library.

Notes

1. If the Periodical Publication is current in the library, the number of the latest volume and its year are to be written in Pencil.

2. If the Periodical Publication is current in the library, the entry is current in the library is said to be "open for the library".
3. If the Periodical Publication is discontinued in the library, the entry is said to be "closed for the library".

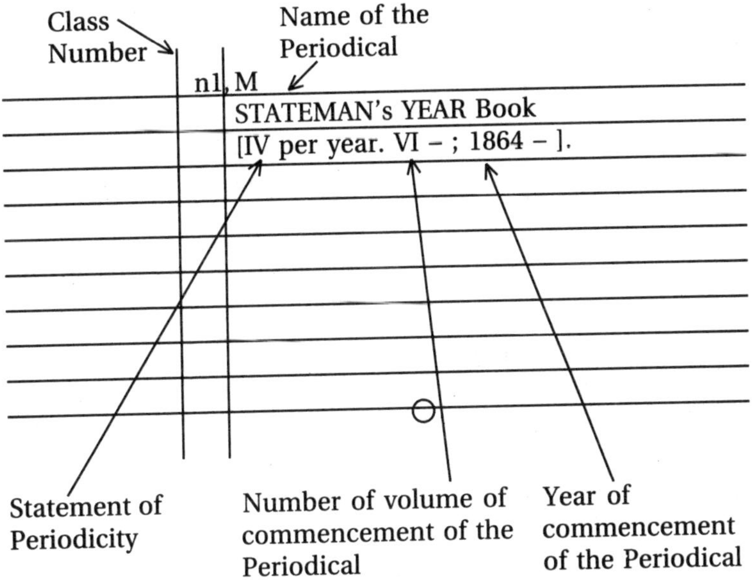

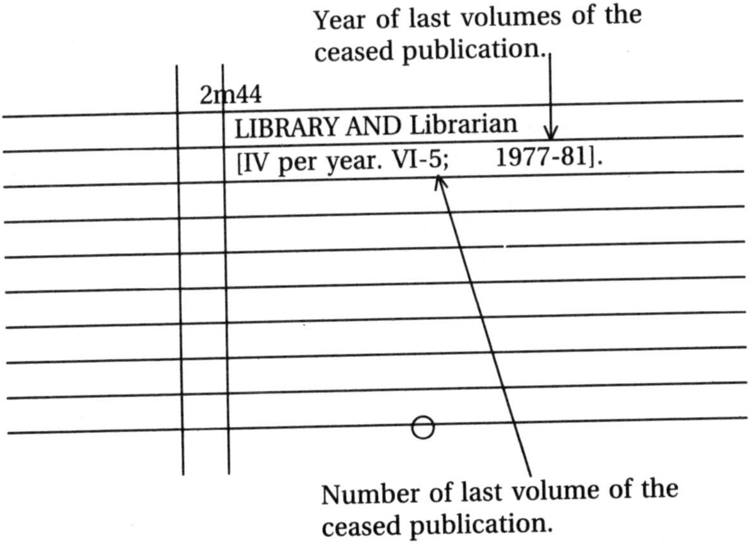

w73rM9

WHO's WHO America.

[IV per year. V1 – ; 1899 –].

This library has V1-86; 1899-2000.

In pencil as publication is continuously received in the library.

According to Dr. Ranganathan the idea in writing the numbers of the volumes and of the year of the latest volumes in pencil, if the periodical publication is current in the library, they will be changed in to the succeeding number as soon as the succeeding volumes gets completed and accessioned.

Discontinued Set

If the library is having discontinued set of the Periodicals, for each continuous block of the set —

1. The information covered is to be written as a single book,
2. The blocks of information so given are to be in the increasing sequence of the numbers of their respective volumes or year,
3. Each block of information so given is to be separated from its succeeding block by a full stop.

Unbroken set

1m56, M8
Annals of Botany.
[IV per year. V1 – ; 1887 –].
This library has V1-47; 1887-1933.

If the year of volume is not a Calendar year

W, 6m44, N3
LOCAL SELF-GOVERNMENT
Quarterly, (Madras Chamber of Local Boards).
[IV per year. VI – ; 1931/32 –].
This library has VI-2; 1931/32 —
1932-33.

In above example the year (Artificial year) spread over two calendar years. It may be from April to March, a financial year or any other sequence of the years *i.e.*:

April to March

October to September

January to December

However, statement of periodicity makes this difference clear.

When the volumes of serial are not numbered

3,441i, t41, Mn
CALENDAR, Presidency College
(Madras).
[IV per year. –]
This library has 1926-1933.

Example : AAUT Bulletin/Vol. 16 (4) / December 1980/ Publication of American Association of University Teachers/ Call Number T4m73, N15. The library has got the complete set except Vol. 10-12, 17-21 and continuing till date.

T4m 73, N15
BULLETIN, American,
Association of University teachers.
[IV per year. VI – ; 1964 –].
This library has VI-9; 1964-72.
V13-16; 1975-8. V22-40; 1984-2002.

in pencil

Class Index Entries (Ordinary)

UNIVERSITY EDUCATION.
For document in this Class and its Subdivisions
see the Classified Part of the catalogue under the
Class Number T4

EDUCATION.

For document in this Class and its Subdivisions see the Classified Part of the catalogue under the Class Number T

Class Index Entry (Specific)

AMERICAN ASSOCIATION OF UNIVERSITY TEACHERS. Bulletin.

T4m 73, N15

AAUT BULLETIN.

T4m 73, N15

Class Index Entry (Generic)

PERIODICAL.

Bulletin, American Association of University Teachers.

T4m 73, N15

PERIODICAL.
American Association of University
Teachers, Bulletin.
T4m73, N15

PERIODICAL, UNIVERSITY EDUCATION.
T4m

TRACING

Tracing of the Headings of Class Index entries and its various kinds, is essentially be made as to facilitate the cataloguer to know, how many added entries are made of the document, other than the main entry.

It is a separate section of the Main Entry. It is prepared on the back of the main card with the hole of the card on upper side. It is to be divided in two parts —

1. Left Half
2. Right Half

LEFT HALF RIGHT HALF

Left Half

There are four informations to be given on the left half in the sequence horizontally :

1. Number – Volume Number
2. Year Number (Year of the volume)
3. Book Number (Book Number of the volume)
4. Accession Number (Accession Number of the volume).

It is to be written in Tabular form using inclusive notation, wherever possible.

Example :

1 1887 M87 2345

Tracing of Main Entry (on back side)

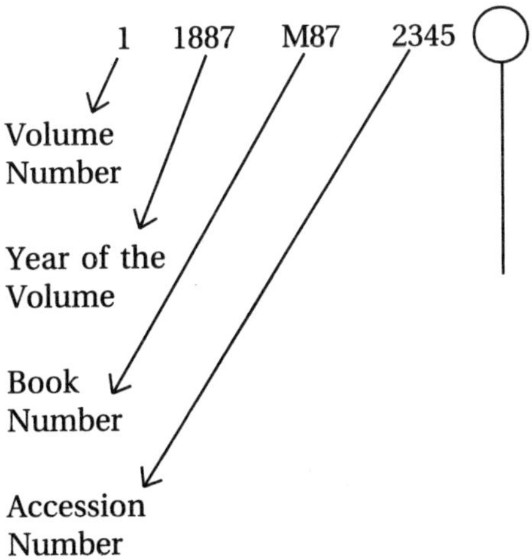

Right Half

On the right half of the Tracing Section the following headings of various Class Index Entries etc. are given —

(A) Call Number used for each Class Reference Entry along with the indication of its Locus.

(B) Heading used for each Class Index Entry :

(i) Class Index Entry (specific)

JOURNAL, sponsoring body. Index Number

SPONSORING BODY, Journal. Index Number

(ii) Class Number Entry (Generic)

(a) PERIODICAL.

Journal, sponsoring body. Index Number

(b) PERIODICAL.

Sponsoring body, Journal. Index Number

(iii) Class Index Entry (optional), if convenient.

(iv) Class Index Entry (ordinary) — Drive out by chain procedure.

(C) Heading used for each class index entry arising out of each Cross Reference Entry.

(D) In case of the proceedings of the periodical conference, the information is to be furnished —

(a) in left half,

(i) Each volume of the conference — Name of the place of the conference between the number of the year and the Book Number.

NOTE

In case the number of lines in Tracing section exceeds the capacity of the back of the main card, the information is to be continued both in the front and the back of the necessary number of continuation cards.

TRACING

Left Half

VI-3	1962-4	N62-N64	467-9
V8	1969	N69	485
V9	1970	N70	4811

Right Half

Library Science.
Periodical, Library Science.
India, Periodical, Library Science.
Sarda Ranganathan Endowment for Library Science, Herald of Library Science.
Herald of Library Science, Sarda Ranganathan Endowment for Library Science.
Periodical.
Periodical.

Example :

Bulletin of the chemical society of India/Volume 37, No. 10, October 1964 / Published by Chemical Society of India.

Other informations — Class Number Em44, N28

Em44, N28
BULLETIN, Chemical Society of
India.
[IV per year. V1 – ; 1928 –].
This library has V1-23; 1928-50.
V27-43; 1954-70. V53-V63-75; 1979-91.
V81-86; 1997-2002.

Class Index Entries (Specific)

BULLETIN, Chemical Society of
India. Em44, N28

CHEMICAL SOCIETY OF JAPAN.
Bulletin. Em44, N28

Class Index Entries (Generic)

PERIODICAL.
Bulletin, Chemical Society of India. Em44, N28

PERIODICAL.
Chemical Society of India, Bulletin. Em44, N28

Class Index Entry (Optional)

JAPAN, PERIODICAL, CHEMISTRY.
Em44

Class Index Entry (Ordinary)

CHEMISTRY.
For document in this Class and its Subdivisions see the Classified Part of the catalogue under the Class Number E

TRACING

1-3	1928-50	N28-N50	472-94	Chemistry.
27-43	1954-70	N54-N70	927-43	Periodical. Chemistry.
63-75	1979-91	N79-N91	958-70	India, Periodical, Chemistry.
81-86	1997-2002	N97-002	982-7	Chemical Society of India, Bulletin
				Bulletin, Chemical Society of India.
				Periodical.
				Periodical.

Cross Reference Entries

No Cross Reference Entry is to be made for Periodical Publications.

CR Entries are to be made only in case of – (exceptions) :

1. If there is a separate volume having special features.
2. If it is a festschrift.
3. If forming a special volume.

Such volume should be treated as simple and ordinary composite book and rendered as follows as a Cross Reference Entries —

1. Leading Section — Class Number as an independent work,
2. Directing element "see", and
3. Class Number of periodical publications,
4. Heading of periodical publications,
5. Locus section in the form,
6. Term V, and
7. Number of the volume or its year or both.

Bp 77N30

See

Bm44, NO

Bulletin, Calcutta Mathematical Society.

V20;1928

Note : It is a commemoration volume.

Class Index Entry (Additional)

Ordinary Class Index Entry is a entry which represent the last link of the Chain, *i.e.* sought link. The heading of the Class Index Entry contributed by the last link of the Class Number of a periodical publication is to be the same as that of its main entry.

If a periodical publication is one associated with another, the link forming the Class Number of the Host Periodical Publication is to be taken as an unsought link.

HERALD of Library Science, (Sarda Ranganathan Endowment for Library Science). 2m44, N62

	SARDA RANGANATHAN ENDOWMENT	
	FOR LIBRARY SCIENCE, Herald	
	of Library Science.	
		2m44, N62

Class Index Entries (Optional)

Sought links other than the last link in the chain of a Class Number are to be considered for Class Index Entries (Additional). In other words the sought links corresponding to the last link of the Class Number of a periodical publications, are written as Additional Class Index Entries.

Such entries are written under the headings without the statement of a ordinary Class Index Entries *i.e.* (for documents...... see the classified part...... under the Class Number.......).

Some other additional headings should also be considered for Additional Class Index Entries such as follows —

1. Every alternative name :
   - (a) Alternative name,
   - (b) Contracted name,
   - (c) Initionym, popularly referred to among its users.
2. In case of sponsoring periodical publications, the heading got by interchanging the name of the sponsor, and the title of the periodical publications.
3. Every variations got by substituting every alternative name of the sponsor in the headings.
4. A comma is inserted as connecting symbol in between sponsoring body and the name of periodical.

INDIA, PERIODICAL, LIBRARY SCIENCE. 2m44

PERIODICAL, LIBRARY SCIENCE.
2m

Class Index Entries (Generic)

Generic Class Index Entrics are written with the Heading "Periodical" or "Serial", as the case may be, corresponding to each of its specific Class Index Entries.

The second and the third sections of Generic Class Index Entry of the periodical publication are to consist, respectively of—

(a) Heading of specific Class Index Entry to which it corresponds, and

(b) The Class Number of the periodical publication.

Class Index Entry (Generic)

PERIODICAL.
Herald of Library Science, (Sarda Ranganathan Endowment for Library Science).
2m44, N62

PERIODICAL.
Sarda Ranganathan Endowment for
Library Science, Herald of Library Science.
2m 44, N62

Ordinary Class Index Entry

Entry which are made as the Main subject of sought heading in the chain.

LIBRARY SCIENCE.
For document in this Class and its Subdivisions
see the Classified Part of the catalogue under the
Class Number 2

Book Index Entries

No Book Index Entry is to be given to a periodical publication. Avoid such headings :

(a) If it is given in Class Index Entries.

(b) Only such headings are given for Book Index Entry, if they are necessary out of Cross Reference Entry.

Cumulative Index

If a volume of a periodical publication constituting a cumulative index, there will be a main entry under the Class Number of such volume with the book number of such volume as follows —

1. Leading section consisting of the Call Number
2. Heading of the periodicals as in Main Entry

3. Extract from the title page, indicating the nature and scope of the index.

		1m 56, M8 bNO1
		Annals of botany.
		Index to V1-10; 1887-96.

Irregularity in Volume Number

If the periodical publication is not regularly published or it is irregular by period, volume number or year or both, a separate main card is to be made for each volume-periodicity in periodicity section.

1. The class number in each such card being the same, all such cards are to be treated as a set of "continued cards".
2. the entry in all but the last card of the set is to be "closed for the publication".

Difference Sequence in Volume Number

There may be three kinds of complexities :

(a) Change in volume-periodicity

(b) Volume being numbered in two or more sequences, the sequence being termed new series, first series, second series etc.

(c) Volume being numbered simultaneously in two or more sequences.

In the above three complexities, a separate main card is to be made for each sequence with the name of its series before the term "V" in the volume periodicity section.

Class Number will be the same. All cards will be in continuation as 'continued' card in a set and the last card will be said to be "closed for publication".

Interrupted Publication

When periodical publication is breaked/withheld for a year or above, but the volume number continued without any break.

Example :

V1 – 5; 1980-5

V6 – 9; 1987-90

V10–16;1993-9

In above example there is a break in years. There is break in year 1986, 1991-2, but there is no break in volume numbers.

In such cases an additional section is to be added in crooked bracket (square bracket) after the holding section.

Example : International Library Progress/Delhi first published in 1978. The publication interrupted in 1987-89 and 1992 but volume number remain continued.

2m 44,N
INTERNATIONAL LIBRARY Progress
(Delhi).
[IV per year. V1 – ; 1978 –].
This library has VI-25; 1978-2002.
{No V in 1987-9, 1992}.

Interrupted publication is a complexity and frequently occurred. It consists the following information while rendering in main entry :

1. It is given in crooked bracket { }
2. After the holding section
3. Term "No V in"; and
4. Years corresponding to which there is no volume.

Many periodicals seem to have suffered an interruption due to —

(a) Casualties

(b) Lack of finance

(c) War

(d) Non-availability of raw material

(e) Mismanagement

(f) Other reasons.

In such cases periodical publication is not published during such years. But few publishers or sponsoring bodies do not break the volume number. They continued the sequence (serial number) of volumes. This caused the interruption or break in years. Hence, there may be —

4 volumes in 5 years

7 volumes in 9 years

e.g.	V1	-	1991
	V2	-	1992
	V3	-	1994
	V4	-	1995
	V5	-	1996
	V6	-	1998
	V7	-	1999
	V8	-	2000
	V9	-	2001
	V10	-	2002
	V11	-	

Example : ISIS started by the History of Science Society (Washington DC) in 1913, had to be suspended from July 1914 to Aug. 1919, with the result, while the 1913 volume is numbered as 1, the volume for 1920 is numbered as 2 instead of 8.

Avm73,N
ISIS, (History of Science Society)
(Washington DC).
[IV per year. V1 – ; 1913 –].
This library has V1-15; 1913-23
{No V in 1914-19}.

J: (E)m 73, N
JOURNAL, Association of Official
Agricultural Chemists (Washington DC).
[IV per year. V1 – ; 1915 –].
This library has V1 – 16; 1915 – 33.
{No V in 1917-9}.

Suspension with break in Volume Number (Irregularity in Publication)

When there is a break in the sequence or irregularity in the numbering of volumes due to non-publication or other causes.

In such cases an Additional Note is to be added in crooked brackets, after the section on periodicity, consisting of —

1. Term "V", either;
2. Numbers of the volumes not published; or
3. Term "for the year(s)"; and
4. Numbers of the years of the volumes not published, and

5. Term "not published".

XX31m73, N
PROCEEDINGS, Certified Milk
Producer's Association of America.
[IV per year. V3 – ; 1920 –].
{V1-2 not published}.
This library has V3-16; 1920-33.

Example : Local Self-Government quarterly/Madras Chamber of Local Boards. It is an Annual publication. Library is receiving volumes regularly. But V5-6 are not published. Class Number. W6m44,N3. It started its publication in 1965.

W6m44, N3
LOCAL SELF Government
Quarterly, (Madras Chamber of
Local Board).
[IV per year. V1 – ; 1965 –].
{V5-6 not published}.
This library has V1-4; 1965-8.
V7-36; 1971-2000.

Volumes Bound Together

If there are two or more volumes published as a single volume or bound as a single volume.

Example :

1. Vol. 7 and 8 published together.
2. Vol. 11 and 12 published separately but bound together.

In case of such complexity, an additional note is to be added in crooked brackets after the section on periodicity, consisting of —

1. Term "published together"

   or

   "bound together" as the case may be.
2. Specification of each set of volumes published or bound together, prescribed by; either.
3. Term "V" followed by the numbers of volumes forming the set.
4. A semi-colon.
5. Years of volumes forming the set; or
6. The year alone if the volumes are not numbered; and a full stop between the successive blocks of such information about the respective sets, if there are two or more sets.

Such type of complexity is generally occurred. When the periodical is published 'half-yearly' and wears few pages, libraries bound 2-3 volumes together to save the money in binding.

On the other hand, when there occurs an abnormal delay in publication of the periodical, the sponsor publish two volumes together to maintain its regularity in volume numbers and the year in future.

Example : In case of publication :

V1 - 1991

V2 - 1992

V3-4 - 1993-4

V5 - 1995

In case of binding :

V6 - 1996 [Vol. 6 and 7, though published

V7 - 1997 separately, but bound together.

Such volumes create complexity in cataloguing.

Em73, N28

BULLETIN, Chemical Society of America (Washington DC).

[IV per year. V1 – ; 1991 –].

{V3-4; 1993-4 published together}.

This library has V1 – 7; 199-7.

2m.44

LIBRARY AND Librarian, (Library Publications) (Agra).

[IV per year. V1 – ; 1976 –].

{V2-3 bound together}.

This library has V1-8; 1976-83.

011,m44, N9:g

JOURNAL OF literacy criticism, Indian Society of English (Bombay).

[IV per year. V1 – ; 1990 –].

{V2-3 bound together}.

{V7-8 published together}.

This library has V1 – 13; 1990-2002.

Change of Title and Sponsor

There are few complexities related to :

1. Change of title :
   (a) Without change in sequence of Volume Number
   (b) With change in sequence of Volume Number.
2. Change of sponsor — without change in sequence of volume number <u>or</u> with change in sequence of volume number.

1. Change of Title. If there is a change in title, a separate main card is to be made for each different title and heading. Class Number being the same, the cards are to be treated as a set of 'continued cards', the entry of last card of the set is to be 'closed for publication'.

The change of title and change in sponsoring body occur rather frequently. There may be any chance when different class numbers may be needed, but the cumulative index helps in avoiding the different class numbers.

Sometimes the change in the name is very slight and imperceptible; sometimes the learned societies themselves appear to be subject to slip of memory.

Example 1 :

	L:	4:7m 44, N9
		BULLETIN, Indian Association
	of	Doctors (Nagpur).
		[IV per year; 1911-13].
		This library has V1-4; 1911-13.
		Continued on the next card

Continued 1

L: 4:7m 44, N9

TRANSACTION, Indian Association of Doctors (Nagpur).

[IV per year; V1–4; 1914-7].

This library has V1–4; 1914-7.

Continued on the next card

Continued 2

L: 4:7m 44, N9

MEDICAL JOURNAL, Indian Association of Doctors (Nagpur).

[IV per year; V5-10; 1918-23].

This library has V5-10; 1918-23.

Continued on the next card

Continued 3

L: 4:7m 44, N9

DOCTORS JOURNAL, Indian Association of Doctors (Nagpur).

[IV per year; V11-27; 1924-40].

This library has V11-27; 1924-40.

Example 2 :

Lm73,M8
PROCEEDINGS, Chicago Medical
Society.
[IV per year. V1-3N10; 1888-91].
This library has V1-3N10; 1888-91.
{V3 not completed}.

Continued on the next card

Lm73:M8
CHICAGO MEDICAL record, (Chicago
Medical Society).
[IV per year. V1-2; 1891-2].
This library has V1-2; 1891-2.

AMALGAMATION

A. Continuation of Title and Volume Number

When two periodical publications join together and one of these finish existence and accept the others publication in its continuous existence without any change in volume number. In such cases —

1. The Class Number of the continuous periodical publication will remain the same as in earlier card.
2. They are to be treated as a set of 'continued cards'.

3. The entries of the main cards of all the amalgamated publications including the earlier one of the continued title, are to be 'closed for publication' and 'closed for the library'.
4. In the new main card an additional note is to be added after the holding section and written within inverted commas, consisting successively of the :
   (a) Term "Amalgamates"; and
   (b) Class Numbers and names of the other periodical publication amalgamated with it, the information about the different publication being put in separate lines.
5. In the last main card of each of the periodical publications mentioned in the Additional note of the new main card, an additional note is to be added after section on periodicity, consisting successively of the —
   (a) Term "Amalgamated with", and
   (b) Class number and the name of the publication with which it is amalgamated.

NOTE

Amalgamations occur fairly frequently. Sometimes they occur without notice and suddenly. Sometimes due notice is given. Or the amalgamation is explicitly brought to the notice of readers at least after the event.

In some cases no such clue is given except for a slight change in the title.

"Does it not seem an unhappy circumstance that such a magazine should lose its identity?....... Since, however it has been decreed that the same and form should vanish, it is most fortunate that the spirit and substance are to be preserved in a journal that has so clearly won its way to educational leadership.

Example :

Periodical-I

Journal of Education India.

Annual. First published in 1911.

Periodical-II

Educational Review. India.

Annual. Started in 1921.

Note : The periodical 'Educational Review' was amalgamated to 'Journal of Education' in 1931 but the volume number remain continued (of Journal of Education).

Main Entry of Journal of Education. India

Tm44, N1

JOURNAL OF Education (India).

[IV per year; V1-21; 1911-32].

This library has V1-21; 1911-32.

Continued in the next card

Tm73, M9

EDUCATIONAL REVIEW (India).

[IV per year; V1-38; 1891-1928].

This library has V1-38; 1891-1928.

"Amalgamated with

Tm73,N1 JOURNAL OF EDUCATION".

Tm44, N1

JOURNAL OF Education (India).

[IV per year; V1-27; 1915-28].

This library has V1-27; 1915-28.

"Amalgamates

Tm73, M9 EDUCATIONAL REVIEW (India)".

Continuation of Title but not of Volume Number

When two periodicals amalgamate *i.e.* one journal amalgamates in the other journal, but the volume number of the periodical, in which amalgamates, are changed and start with volume 1 or the other sequence as per decision of the sponsoring body of the periodical in which one periodical is amalgamated.

Example : There are two periodicals in library science and being published smoothly for the last 20 years. But due to some reasons one of the periodical failed to enable its continuity of publication and decided to amalgamate with the other periodical.

Periodical – I	Periodical – II
Library Science Bulletin	**Library Science Service**
First published in 1985	First published in 1982
Library is subscribing regularly	Library is subscribing regularly.
It is a annual periodical	It is a Annual periodical.
This periodical amalgamated with Library Science Service.	This periodical amalgamates with Library Science Bulletin
	The volume number of the Periodical 'Library Science Bulletin' did not continued.

2m44
LIBRARY SCIENCE Bulletin (India).
[IV per year; V1-8; 1985-92].
This library has V1-8; 1985-92.
"Amalgamated with
2:3m44 LIBRARY SCIENCE SERVICE
(India)".

2:3m44
LIBRARY SCIENCE Service (India).
[IV per year; V1-11; 1982-92].
This library has V1-11; 1982-92.

2:3m44
LIBRARY SCIENCE Service (India).
[IV per year; V1-11; 1982-92].
This library has V1-21; 1982-2002.
"Amalgamates
2m44 LIBRARY SCIENCE Bulletin
(India)".

New Title and Old Class Number

New title may be given new main card. If the class number is the same as far the earlier title whose numbering of volumes is continued under the new titles, it is to be treated.

New Title and New Class Number

A new title is to be given in main card.

1. An additional note is to be added in it, within inverted commas, consisting successively of the :
   (a) Term "Amalgamates"; and
   (b) Class Numbers and the titles of the periodical publications amalgamated in it, the informations about the different publications being put in separate lines.
2. The entries of the main cards of all the amalgamated publications are to be 'closed for the publication' are 'closed for the library'.
3. An additional note is to be added, within inverted commas in the last main card of each of the Amalgamated Publications, consisting successively of the :
   (a) Term "Amalgamated in", and
   (b) Class Number and the title of publication Amalgamating it.

Gm73,N
BIOLOGICAL ABSTRACTS.
[IV per year; V1- ; 1927-].
This library has V1-7; 1927-33.
"Amalgamates
G91am73, N ABSTRACTS OF
Bacteriology; and
4am73, N BOTANICAL ABSTRACTS".

G91am,N

ABSTRACT ON Bacteriology.

[IV per year; V1-10; 1917-26].

This library has V1-10; 1917-26.

"Amalgamated in

Gam73,N BIOLOGICAL ABSTRACTS".

1am73,N

BOTANICAL ABSTRACTS.

[IV per year; V1-7; 1912-26].

This library has V1-7; 1912-26.

"Amalgamated in

Gam73,N BIOLOGICAL ABSTRACTS".

SPLITTING UP COMPLEXITY

Each of the publications into which the original is split is to be given a new main card.

1. The old main card and the main card of the publication continuing the old class number are to be treated as a set of "continued cards".
2. The entry in the old main card is to be 'closed for publication' and also 'closed for the library'.
3. An additional note is to be added within inverted commas, in its old main card, consisting successively of the :

(a) Term "split partially into", and

(b) Class number and the title of each of the publications, other than the one continuing the old class number, into which it is split, the information about each publication being given in a separate.

4. In the main card of each of the publications, other than the one continuing the old class number, into which it is split, an additional note is to be added within inverted commas, consisting, successively of the :

(a) Term "split partially from", and

(b) Class number and the title of the original publications.

Example : Journal of Chemistry, Italy. It is regular. It spitted in two periodicals :

1. Journal General Chemistry Published Section-A
2. Journal of Organic Soil. Section-B

Class Number Original & 1 = Cm, N75m52.2.J:1,35m.62,N9

	Cm52,N75
	JOURNAL OF Chemistry, (Chemical
	Society) (Italy).
	[IV per year. V1-10; 1982-91].
	This library has V1-10; 1982-91.
	"Split partially into
	J:1, 35m52, N9 JOURNAL OF Chemistry
	(Chemical Society) (Italy),
	Section B. Chemical soil".
	Continued in the next card

Cm52, N75
JOURNAL OF Chemistry, (Chemical Society) (Italy).
[IV per year. V11-50; 1962-91].
This library has V11-50; 1962-91.

J:1, 35m52, N9
JOURNAL OF Chemistry, (Chemical Society) (Italy), Section B, Chemical soil.
[IV per year. V1-10; 1962-91].
This library has V1-10; 1962-91.
<u>"Split partially from</u>
Cm52,N75 JOURNAL OF Chemistry, (Chemical Society) (Italy).

Class Number continued by None

This complexity is to be treated on analogy of Section PG1 (CCC) and its subdivisions, with the modification that the term "split" is to be substituted for the term "split partially" wherever it occurs.

Am42,M

JOURNAL, College of Science,
Imperial University of Tokyo.
[Irregular. V1-45; 1887-1925].
This library has V1-45; 1887-1925.
"Split into
BZm42, N2 JOURNAL, Faculty of Science,
Imperial University of Tokyo, Section 1.
Hm42,N2 JOURNAL, Faculty of Science,
Imperial University of Tokyo, Section 2".

Continued in the next card

Continued

Am42M

JOURNAL, College of Science, Imperial
University of Tokyo.
1m42, N2 JOURNAL, Faculty of Science,
Imperial University of Tokyo, Section 3.

Card-2

BZm 42,N2

JOURNAL, Faculty of Science,
Imperial University of Tokyo, Section
Mathematics, Astronomy, Physics, Chemistry.
[Irregular. V1- ; 1925 -].
This library has V1- ; 1925 - .
"Split from
Am42,M JOURNAL, Faculty of Science,
Imperial University of Tokyo".

Card-3

```
Hm42,N2
    JOURNAL, Faculty of Science,
Imperial University of Tokyo, Section
2 Geology, Mineralogy, Geography, Seismology
    [Irregular. V1-  ; 1925 -    ].
    This library has V1-2; 1925-1926.
    "Split from
    Am42,M JOURNAL, Faculty of Science,
Imperial University of Tokyo".
```

Card-4

```
1m42,N2
    JOURNAL, Faculty of Science,
Imperial University of Tokyo, Section
3 Botany
    [Irregular. V1-  ; 1925 -    ].
    This library has V1-4; 1925-1932.
    "Split from
    Am42,M JOURNAL, Faculty of Science,
Imperial University of Tokyo".
```

Splitting into Independent Periodicals

When a periodical publication split into independent periodicals and lost the existence of original periodical, this complexity is treated as follows —

1. The term "split on completion of each volume into" is to be substituted for the term "split".
2. The entry of original periodical will not have the holding section.
3. The original periodical will cease to exist when the volume is completed.

4. The independent periodical is given a note, consisting of the —
   (a) Term "originally published as part of", and
   (b) Class Number and the title of the publication of which it was originally a part.

Example : Abgila has three parts —

1. Annals
2. Bulletin
3. Granthalaya

Full name of Abgila. Annals, Bulletin, Granthalaya of Indian Library Association.

The periodical publication Abgila split into independent periodicals entitled as —

1. Annals, Indian Library Association
2. Bulletin, Indian Library Association
3. Granthalaya, Indian Library Association

All these three journals have separate entity and existence though sponsored by one body *i.e.* Indian Library Association.

The entry will be as under —

Independent parts

2m44,N4,2

ANNALS, Indian Library Association

[IV per year. V3- ; 1953].

This library has V3 ; 1953.

"Originally published as part of

2m44,N4,4 ABGILA, (Indian Library

Association)".

2m44,N4,3

BULLETIN, Indian Library Association
[IV per year. V3, N2; 1953, March, June].
This library has V3, N2; 1953 March, June].
<u>"Originally published as part of</u>
2m44,N4,4 ABGILA, (Indian Library
Association)".

2m44,N4,4

GRANTHALAYA (Indian Library Association).
[IV per year. V3,N2; 1953, March, June].
This library has V3,N2; 1953, March, June.
<u>"Originally published as part of</u>
2m44,N4,4 ABGILA, (Indian Library
Association)".

2m44,N4,1

ABGILA (Indian Library Association).
[IV per year. V3– ; 1953].
<u>"Split on completion of each volume</u>
<u>Into</u>
2m44,N4,2 ANNALS, Indian
Library Association.
2m44,N4,3 BULLETIN, Indian
Library Association.
2m44N4,4 GRANTHALAYA, I.L.A."

Dependent Parts

2m44,N4,2

ANNALS, Indian Library Association.

[IV in 2 years. V1-2; 1949-52].

This library has V1-2; 1949-52.

2m44,N4,3

BULLETIN, Indian Library Association.

[IV per year. V1-2; 1949-52].

This library has V1-2 ; 1949-52.

2m44,N4,4

GRANTHALAYA, (Indian Library Association).

[IV in 2 years. V1-2; 1949-52].

This library has V1-2 ; 1949-52.

Supplement

If there is a supplement of a book or monograph but it has —

1. Separate pagination and title page.
2. No separate pagination and the title page.
3. Separate pagination and the title page but regarded as a periodical publication by itself.
4. A cumulative index of the main periodical publication.

1. With separate pagination. In such cases —

(a) Each monograph supplement or book supplement is to be separated from the periodical publication.

(b) It is dealt with the independent book.

(c) In the main card of the monograph and the book, an additional note is to be added within inverted commas, consisting of the :

(i) Term "for supplement see".

(ii) Call Numbers of the separate book (supplement).

(d) In the main card of the separate book (supplement), an appropriate extract note is to be added.

(e) If a supplement of this kind chances to be bound with a volume of the periodical publication, it is to be dealt with as bound volume.

Card-1

z44m44, N27
JOURNAL OF Oriental Research.
[IV per year. 1 - ; 1927 -].
This library has V1-7; 1927-33.
"For supplements see
P31, Dx1, 1 N30,1
015, 2D35, V N31
R641 x 4, 3 15N32".

Card-2

P31, Dx1, 1 N30.1
TOLKAPPNAM.... Ed with comm..
in English by PS Subramaniya Shastri.
V.1. Eluttatikarani
(Madras Oriental series. 3).
"Supplement to
z44m44,N27 JOURNAL OF
Oriental Research. V2-4; 1928-30".

61618

Card-3

015, 2D35, V N31
BHASA.
Vinavasavadattam with introd. by
K Kuppuswami Sastri.
(Madras Oriental series, 2).
"Supplement to
{44m44,N27 JOURNAL OF
Oriental Research. V1,3-5;1922, 1929-31".

61617

R641x4,V 15 N32
MISRA (Mandan).
Vibhramavieveka. Ed. by S. Kappuswami
Sastri and TV Ramchandra Dikshitar.
(Madras Oriental series, 1).
"Supplement to
z44m44,N27 JOURNAL OF
Oriental Research. V1; 1927".

61616

Supplementary Periodical Publication

In such complexities, the supplement are to be treated as Independent periodical publications as additional note is to be added within inverted commas, consisting of the —

1. Term "Has as supplement"; and
2. Class Numbers and the titles of the supplements, the information about such supplement being given in separate lines.
3. In the main card of supplements, an additional note is to be added within inverted commas, consisting of the—
   (a) Term "supplement to"; and
   (b) Class number and title of the main publication.

CUMULATIVE INDEX

If the supplements are treated as separate periodical publications or separate books, are covered/contains by the Cumulative Indexes of the main periodical publications.

Supplement } as separate periodical publication } Covered by Cumulative Index of Main Periodical

OR

Supplement – as separate book – covered by cumulative index of main periodical

Such Cumulative Index are provided with a Class Numbers or the call number, of the separate supplements.

Volumes bound together

There have been some journals which have less frequency. These are periodical publications which are published twice a year or quarterly and contains 30 or forty pages. On the other hand libraries have paucity of funds for binding. Moreover, sometimes libraries decide to bound two volumes together as a policy matter.

In such cases the entry will consists the following informations in note section :

1. In the main entry of the periodical publication bound with other volume and found the sequence among others, a note will be given in note section "Bound together".
2. Volume numbers bound along with their years.

Bm44,N
JOURNAL, Indian Mathematical Society.
[IV per year. V3-14; 1911-22].
This library has V3-14; 1911-22.
{Bound together V3-4; 1911-12, V5-6;
1913-14. V7-8; 1915-6. V9-10; 1917-8; V11-12;
1919-20. V13-14; 1931-2}.

PERIODICAL PUBLICATIONS

Combination of Complexity

If there occur more complexities in the periodical publications, these may be worked out and shown in Note-section.

It may be recalled that the following kinds of sections and notes are possible :

1. Section on periodicity, enclosed in square brackets.
2. Series note, enclosed in circular brackets.
3. Holding section, not enclosed in any way.
4. Complexity note, enclosed in crooked brackets; and
5. Notes relating to 'Amalgamation', 'split up', and 'supplement' each enclosed within inverted commas.

The information of complexity, sections and notes are given in different cards —

1. First card. All appropriate sections and notes, in first card and in each of the continued cards.

2. First section. The section on periodicity is to be the first section after the Title Section.

3. Last section. The holding section will be the last section, in each card.

4. Complexity notes. Complexity notes are to be written after the holding section, in their chronological sequence.

5. Separate section. Each note is to be written as a separate section.

Example 1 :

Am56, K.1

ABSTRACT OF the papers printed in the......... transactions, Royal Society (London).

[Irregular. V1-6; 1800-1850/54].

This library has V1-6; 1800/14-1850/54.

Continued on the next card

Split in to two periodical publications

Am56,k,1 Continued 2

PROCEEDINGS Royal Society (London)

[Irregular. V7-75; 1856/57-1904-5.

"Split into

Azm56,k, 1 Proceedings, Series A, Royal Society (London).

Gm56,K,1 Proceedings, series B, Royal Society (London)".

Azm56,k,1

PROCEEDINGS Series A, Royal Society (London).

[Irregular. V76 - ; 1905 -].

This library has V115-142; 1927-33.

"Split from

Am56,k,1 PROCEEDINGS, Royal Society (London)".

Gm56,k,1
PROCEEDINGS Series B, Royal Society (London).
[Irregular. V76 - ; 1905 -].
This library has V75-142; 1905/6-1927/33.
"Split from
Am56,k,1 PROCEEDINGS, Royal Society (London)".

Example 2 :

Bm44,N
JOURNAL, Indian Mathematical Society.
[IV for two years. V3- ; 1911-].
This library has V3-19; 1911-1931/32.
"Each V from V/6 has as supplement
Bp44,N REPORT, Indian Mathematical Conference".

Bp44,N
REPORT, Indian Mathematical Conference.
[IV for two years. V4 - ; 1924 -].
This library has V5-7; 1924-31.
{V4 and 5 bound with Bm44, N JOURNAL, Indian Mathematical Society,V15&16 respectively}.

Continued on the next card

Bp44,N Continued...2

REPORT, Indian Mathematical Conference.

[VI-3 not separately published, but included in

Bm44,N JOURNAL, Indian Mathematical

Society, V9,11 and 13}.

"Supplement to

Bm 44,1N JOURNAL, Indian Mathematical

Society".

30

UNION CATALOGUE

It is a list of all the documents in two or more libraries giving the names of all the libraries where copies of each document can be found. A union catalogue may cover all kinds of documents or any restricted kind of them.

A union catalogue may be of libraries of a —

1. Country
2. Zone
3. Locality

The location detail is given in the main entry of a book, in which library, the book is having its physical entry. This information is given in the Holding Section of the main entry. Every library is allotted a code number.

<u>The Holding Section</u> is kept up-to-date if —

1. Each participating library has to inform the union catalogue center of each of the new book accessioned from time to time.
2. Each participating library has to inform the union catalogue center of each of the old book weeded out from time to time.
3. The holding section may be updated either by sending the list periodically or by sending the duplicate copy of the main card or its photocopy.

In fact it is seldom that union catalogue center finds the information from participating libraries time to time. This difficulty arises on both the parts. Participating libraries are not careful of sending the information while the union catalogue center is under staff to collect all such information from time to time. As a result holding section is invariably left in arrears. Moreover, there is no effective mechanism to make the information up to date.

Area. One must be careful to select the area of union catalogue. The smaller the area, the greater the chances for the union catalogue to be kept up-date.

1. No. of libraries is growing and even more than area, it is the number of participating libraries that really counts.
2. The optimum area for a union catalogue of books depends upon the state of the library development of a country.

Type of Books

The smaller the quantity of different books to be covered by the union catalogue, the greater the chances, for the union catalogue to be kept up-to-date.

A union catalogue may be prepared of any type of the following books —

1. Costly books. The books which may have cost above a minimum.

2. Foreign Language books. Books which are written in foreign languages or the zone and have importance.

3. Advance books. These are treaties, agreements, commissions report, conference proceedings, classic in quality and books likely to be only of occasional use, books which are used by specialist readers.

Such books are generally uneconomic for the purpose of library services.

4. Rare books. Books owned only by a few libraries and not procurable from the market – *i.e.* incunabula.

5. Other valuable books produced in limited number.

Effective Organisation

A effective organisation can minimize the coverage at National and International levels. This target may be achieved by —

1. Supply of printed catalogue cards, one master card for the library and punched cards to the various libraries.

2. Efficient staff should be engaged.
3. Quantitative data may be available.
4. Qualitative data should be produced.
5. Sufficient finance should be available.

Pre-Natal Cataloguing

Pre-Natal cataloguing can make easy the work of union catalogue — National central libraries should adopt Pre-Natal cataloguing with one language or by the zonal or state central libraries of a polyglot country. It will make the union catalogue easy and prompt and restricted to a certain level.

If all National libraries or state libraries of all countries go for preparing Pre-Natal cataloguing and keep cooperation and coordination among them, it make the task of union catalogue more easy and effective.

Cataloguing Rules and Union Catalogue

Union catalogue is a location list of books to know the whereabouts of a book in the area, or locality and the name of the library where it is located. This information is necessary and useful to —

1. The readers of serious nature.
2. The research scholars who are always in search of new books and variety of reading material.
3. Coordinate the book selection.
4. Supplying bibliographical informations.
5. Answering other questions usually asked of the catalogue of a service library.
6. It is economical if used by maximum number of readers and participation by a big number of libraries.
7. It serves a reference tool.

Approach

Union catalogue has many approaches particularly the Author and the title. Generally if it is a service library or enquiry of readers. Therefore, the approach is a dictionary catalogue.

Union catalogue is somewhat different from the rules of catalogue code. It has following categories of informations —

1. Main entry,
2. Holding section of the main entry,
3. Design of library number to be used in heading section,
4. In case of centralized cataloguing, unit catalogue cards of a book bearing author, title are needed.
5. Being a dictionary form of catalogue, and even there to its restriction to author and title entries only, it is a proper finding list. It needs simplest system of alphabetization. Swiss Union Catalogue Centre has advocated the simplification of entry element. It recommended the word-by-word system.

Example :

Maier	Maiyer
Majer	Maiyer
Mayer	Maier
Mayr	

It is useful because —

1. It has more potency in alphabetization.
2. Words have accuracy for enquiry.

But it is a delayed method as it causes delay in the location and any in accuracy may cause confusion.

Card Form

Card form is a suitable form, cards are kept in union catalogue center. Duplicate set may be kept in certain regional centers. Which will be a small set.

Main Entry of Union Catalogue

The main entry of union catalogue consists of —

1. Leading section
2. Title section
3. Holding section

1. Leading section. It consists of — The heading chosen (as per rules applied to other books in CCC-MD).

2. Title Section (as per rules applied to other books in CCC-MD).

3. Holding Section. It consists of —

(a) Library Number (code allotted to each participating libraries).

(b) Library number are arranged in columns with space with them for the mark.

(c) A distinctive mark is to be put in pencil against the library number of the library reporting the accession of a copy of the book.

(d) Report of withdrawal.

Whenever a library reports the withdrawal of a book, the mark against its library number is to be erased.

4. Artificial composite book/multi-volumed book.

In both the cases, the union catalogue center is to prepare a separate main entry for each of its volumes.

Library Numbers

The library numbers are to be constructed on the principle of Geographical contiguity —

(a) Type of library

(b) Subject of specialization

1. Zone Number. The first digit represents the zone of the area of the Union catalogue in which the library is located.

Example :

A	Madras
C	Mysore
E	Maharashtra
H	Rajasthan
M	Uttar Pradesh
S	Assam
T	Orissa

2. Sub-Zone Number. The second digit of library number is to represent the sub-region, comprising one or more districts (countries), in which the library is located. It is call sub-zone number.

Example :

1	East
2	South
3	West
4	North

These numbers may be extended *i.e.* South East, North East, West East, East East.

Chinglepet = Al

Agra = M3

3. Locality Number. The third digit or digit group of a library number is to represent the locality in which library is located. It is called locality number.

The locality number is to be got by the alphabetical device, using capital for the initial letters and smalls for the second and later letters needed for use.

4. Type Number. The fourth digit is to represent the status or the subject of specialization, if any. This may be called the Type Number.

Example :
1 State Central Library
2 Public Library
3 School Library
4 College Library
5 University Library
6 Museum Library
7 Research Institute Library
8 Business or Departmental Library

5. Individualising Number. If there be more than one library with the same library number in the same locality, a further digit – say 1, 2 .... – may be added to individualise them. The further digit may be called individualising number.

AIMI	Madras State Central Library
AIMUI	Presidency College Library
AIMZI	High Court Library
BITS	Kerala University Library
CIBKX	Indian Dairy Research Institute Library.

6. Guide to Library Number. Union catalogue center is to maintain a key to Library Number in two parts as follows :

(a) The first part is to serve as a dictionary to pass from the library number to the name of the library.

(b) The second part is to serve as a dictionary to pass from the name of the library to the library number.

PART – III

PRACTICAL EXAMPLES

31

Practical Examples

Example 1

A GUIDE

TO

EARTH HISTORY

RECHARD CARRINGTON

1956

CHATTO & WINDUS
LONDON

Other information

Call Number H2 J6

Accession Number 15749

Main Entry

H2 J6

CARRINGTON (Rechard).

Guide to earth history.

15749

Class Index Entry

PETROLOGY.

For document in this Class and its Subdivisions, see the Classified Part of the catalogue under the Class Number H2

GEOLOGY.

For document in this Class and its Subdivisions, see the Classified Part of the catalogue under the Class Number H

Book Index Entry

CARRINGTON (Rechard).
Guide to Earth history.
H2 J6

Tracing

Petrology.
Geology.
Carrington (Rechard).

Problem : *Single Author* : Honorific words are avoided

CATALOGUING   **By** **Dr. C.K. Sharma** **M.A., M.Lib., Ph.D.** **Agra University Library** **Agra**   **Shree Publishing Housing** **4056, Ajmeri Gate, Delhi.**

Other information

Call Number 2 : 55 N84

Acc. No. 235

Main Entry

2 : 55 N84
SHARMA (CK).
Cataloguing.

Tracing

○ Cataloguing, Library Science.
Cataloguing.
Sharma (CK).

Class Index Entry

CATALOGUING, LIBRARY SCIENCE.
For document in this Class and its Subdivisions, see the Classified Part of the catalogue under the Class Number 2:55

LIBRARY SCIENCE.
For document in this Class and its Subdivisions, see the Classified Part of the catalogue under the Class Number 2

JAWAHAR LAL NEHRU

GLIMPSES

OF

WORLD HISTORY

With 50 maps

Asia Publishing House
Bombay, Calcutta, New Delhi

Other information

Call Number V1 K2

Acc. No. 1934

The Author was born in the year 1889 and died in 1964. It is second edition.

Main Entry

V44, 21 K2
NEHRU (Jawaharlal) (1889-
1964).
Glimpses of World History. Ed 2.

1934

Class Index Entry

PRIME MINISTER, INDIA, HISTORY.
For document in this Class and its Subdivisions,
see the Classified Part of the catalogue under the
Class Number V44,21

INDIA, HISTORY.
For document in this Class and its Subdivisions,
see the Classified Part of the catalogue under the
Class Number V44

HISTORY
For document in this Class and its Subdivisions, see the Classified Part of the catalogue under the Class Number V

NEHRU (Jawaharlal) (1889-1964).
Glimpses of world history.
Ed 2.
V44, 21k2

GLIMPSES OF World history.
Ed 2.
By Nehru.
V44, 21K2

Cross Reference Index Entry

JAWAHAR LAL NEHRU.
<u>See</u>
NEHRU (Jawaharlal).

Tracing

○

PRIME MINISTER, INDIA, HISTORY.

INDIA, HISTORY.

HISTORY.

Nehru (Jawaharlal).

Glimpses of World History.

Jawahar Lal Nehru.

Physics Series. No. 11
Editor : L. Freeman, M. Berwick

ADVANCED QUANTUM THEORY

BY
GEORGE EDINBURGE

4th EDITION

JAMES – LEE
LONDON
1987

Other informations

Call No. CN1 N1
Acc. No. 3659
Page : XXII, 337
Size 23cm.
ISBN 2-523-23591
Colour plates 7

Main Entry

CN1 N1
EDINBURGE (George).
Advance Quantum theory. Ed. 4.
(Physics series. Ed by L Freeman
and M Berwick. 11).

3659

Tracing

Quantum theory, physics.
Physics.
Edinburge (George)
Advanced Quantum Theory.
Physics Series.

Freeman (L) and
Berwick (M), Ed.
Berwick (M) and
Freeman (L), Ed.

Class Index Entry

QUANTUM THEORY, PHYSICS.
For document in this Class and its Subdivisions,
see the Classified Part of the catalogue under the
Class Number CN1

PHYSICS.
For document in this Class and its Subdivisions, see the Classified Part of the catalogue under the Class Number C

Book Index Entry (Author)

EDINBURGE (George).
Advance Quantum theory.
Ed. 4. CN1 N1

Book Index Entry (Title)

ADVANCED QUANTUM Theory.
Ed. 4.
By Edinburge.
CN1 N1

Series Index Entry

PHYSICS SERIES.
11 Edinburge: Advance Quantum
Theory. CN1 N1

Cross Reference Index Entry (Editor Series).

FREEMAN (L) and BERWICK (M), Ed.
See
PHYSICS SERIES.

BERWICK (M) and FREEMAN (L), Ed.
See
PHYSICS SERIES.

Problem : *Personal author* : Variant forms with collaborators

THE SHORT NOVELS

OF

TOLSTOY

Edited by

PHILIP RAHV

Translated by

AYLMER MAUDE

THE DIAL PRESS
NEW YORK

Other informations

Call Number : 0142, 3M28x H8

Acc. No. : 1298

The original Russian name of the author is Lew Nikolaevich Tolstoi (1928-1910). Full name is Leo Tolstoy.

Main Entry

0142,3M28x H8

TOLSTOY (Leo) (1828-1910).

Short novels. Ed by Philip Rohv;

Tr by Aylmer Maude.

1298

Class Index Entry

WORKS, TOLSTOY (Leo) (1828-1910).

For document in this Class and its Subdivisions, see the Classified Part of the catalogue under the Class Number 0142,3M28x

Class Index Entry

TOLSTOY (Leo), FICTION, RUSSIAN.

For document in this Class and its Subdivisions, see the Classified Part of the catalogue under the Class Number 0142,3m28

FICTION, RUSSIAN.

For document in this Class and its Subdivisions, see the Classified Part of the catalogue under the Class Number 0142

RUSSIAN LITERATURE.

For document in this Class and its Subdivisions, see the Classified Part of the catalogue under the Class Number 0142

LITERATURE.

For document in this Class and its Subdivisions, see the Classified Part of the catalogue under the Class Number 0

Book Index Entry

RAHV (Philip), Ed.

Tolstoy: Short Novels.class.

0142, 3m28x 48

MAUDE (Aylmer), Tr.
Tolstoy: Short novels.
0142, 3M28x H8

Cross Reference Index Entry

TOLSTOI (Lew Nikolaevich) (1828-1910).
See
TOLSTOY (Leo) (1828-1910).

Tracing

Works TOLSTOY (Leo).
(1828-1910)

Tolstoy (Leo), Fiction,
Russian.

Russian Literature.
Literature.

Rahv (Philip), Ed.
Maude (Aylmer), Tr.

Tolstoi (Lew Nikolaevich)
(1828-1910)

Problem : Joint Authors / Series

CATALOGUING OF PERIODICALS IN UNIVERSITY LIBRARY BY R. Luxemburg – N.I. Bokharin University of California Second Edition ACADEMIC PRESS NEWYORK 1971

Other informations

Cataloguing Research Series. 21.

Call No. 234; 46 : 55 N71

Page. x, 291

Size 22cm.

Acc. No. 2234

ISBN 0-23-12732i-1

Main Entry

234; 46:55 N71
LUXEMBURG (R) and BOKHARIN
(N 1).
Cataloguing of periodicals in University
Library. Ed 2.
(Cataloguing Research Series. 21).

2234

Tracing

Cataloguing, Periodicals, University
Library, Library Science.

Periodicals, University Library,
Library Science.

University Library, Library Science.
Library Science.

Luxemburg (R) and Bokharin (N1)
Bokharin (N1) and Luxemburg (R).
Cataloguing Research Service.

Class Index Entry

CATALOGUING, PERIODICAL, UNIVERSITY
LIBRARY, LIBRARY SCIENCE.
For document in this Class and its Subdivisions,
see the Classified Part of the catalogue under the
Class Number 234;46:55

PERIODICAL, UNIVERSITY LIBRARY,
LIBRARY SCIENCE.
For document in this Class and its Subdivisions, see the Classified Part of the catalogue under the Class Number 234;46

UNIVERSITY LIBRARY, LIBRARY SCIENCE.
For document in this Class and its Subdivisions, see the Classified Part of the catalogue under the Class Number 234

LIBRARY SCIENCE
For document in this Class and its Subdivisions, see the Classified Part of the catalogue under the Class Number 2

Author Index Entry

LUXEMBURG (R) and BOKHARIN (N1).
Cataloguing of periodicals in University Library. 234;46:55 N71

Jt. Author Index Entry

BOKHARIN (N1) and LUXEMBURG (R).
Cataloguing of periodicals in University
Library. 234;46:55 N71

CATALOGUING RESEARCH SERIES.
Luxemburg and Bokharin: Cataloguing of
Periodicals in University Library.
234; 46: 55 N71

Problem : More than two authors and collaborators

HUMAN RELATIONS **The Human aspect of Administration.** **By** **Prof. A.M. Whitehall** **Late Prof. A.L. Moore** **Translated by** **A.C. Miller** **&** **Jacob Miller** **Ed. Fourth Revised** **Prentice Hall Inc.** **New York** **1957**

Call No. : X:97 J7

Acc. No. : 381

It is a publication number 9 in Prentice Hall Industrial Relations and Personal series.

Main Entry

```
X  97     J7
   WHITE HALL (AM) and MOORE (AL).
   Human Relations: The Human aspect
of administration. Rev ed 4. Tr by Miller
(AC) and Miller (Jacob).
   (Prentice Hall Industrial Relations
and Personal series).



381
```

Tracing

Industrial relations,
    Economics.
Economics.
Whitehall (AM) and Moore
    (AL).
Moore (AL) and Whitehall
    (AM).
Miller (AC) and Miller
    (Jacob).
Miller (Jacob) and Miller
    (AC).
Human Relation: The aspect
    of administration.
Prentice Hall Industrial
    relation and personal series.

Author Book Index Entries

```
WHITE HALL (AM) and MOORE (AL).
   Human relations: The Human aspect
of administration. Rev ed 4.
                          X:97 J7
```

Jt. Author B.I. Entry

MOORE (AL) and WHITEHALL (AM).
Human relations: The Human aspect of administration. X:97 J7

Collaborator B.I. Entry (Tr.)

MILLER (AC) and MILLER (Jacob), Tr.
Whitehall and Moore: Human relations. The Human aspect of administration.
X : 97 J7

MILLER (Jacob) and MILLER (AC), Tr.
Whitehall and Moore: Human relations : The Human aspect of administration.
X : 97 J7

Series B.I. Entry

PRENTICE HALL INDUSTRIAL RELATIONS
AND PERSONAL SERIES.
9 Whitehall and Moore : Human relations:
The Human aspect of administration.
X : 97 J7

Title B.I. Entry

HUMAN RELATIONS: The Human
aspect of administration.
By Whitehall and Moore.
X:97 J7

Problem : More than two personal authors

Physical and Biological Science Research Monographs

ORBIT OF SUN

Ramesh Tambi	**P Motiwala**
R C Bali	**Raman Dahia**

New Delhi
Aditya Prakashan
1961

Other informations

Call Number : B93:72

Acc. No. : 2315

This is publication number 8 in series. It is second edition.

Main Entry

B93: 73
TAMBI (Ramesh) and others.
Orbit of Sun. Ed. 2.
(Physical and Biological Science
Research Monograph. 8).

2315

Tracing

Orbit, Sun Astronomy
Sun, Astronomy.
Astronomy.

Tambi (Ramesh) and
others.
Physical and Biological
Science Research
Series

Author Index Entry

TAMBI (Ramesh) and others.
Orbit of Sun.
B93:72

ORBIT, SUN, ASTRONOMY.

For document in this Class and its Subdivisions, see the Classified Part of the catalogue under the Class Number B 93 : 72

SUN, ASTRONOMY.

For document in this Class and its Subdivisions, see the Classified Part of the catalogue under the Class Number B93:72

ASTRONOMY.

For document in this Class and its Subdivisions, see the Classified Part of the catalogue under the Class Number B93:72

PHYSICAL AND BIOLOGICAL SCIENCE RESEARCH MONOGRAPH.

8 Tambi and others: Orbit of sun.

B 93 : 72

Problem : More than two authors

Political Science Series. II

FUNCTIONS
OF
PARLIAMENT
IN
INDIA

By

R.K. Sharma	**P.K. Mohanty**
N.K. Singh	**Ram Narain**

Editors

H. Gulani	**Pintoo Chowdhary**
Mohan Singh	

Revised edition Second

STAR PUBLICATIONS
Cuttack (India)
1959

Other informations

Class Number : V44, 31:3 N59

Acc. No. : 3134

Page VI, 312

Size : 22cm.

Main Entry

V44, 31:3 N59
SHARMA (RK) and others.
Functions of Parliament in India.
Rev ed 2. Ed by H Gulani and others.
(Political Science Series. 11).

3134

Tracing

Functions, Parliament, India.
Parliament, India.
India.
Sharma (RK) and others.
Gulani (H) and others, Ed.

Political Science Series.

Class Index Entries

FUNCTIONS, PARLIAMENT, INDIA.
For document in this Class and its Subdivisions, see the Classified Part of the catalogue under the Class Number V44, 31:3 N59

PARLIAMENT, INDIA.

For document in this Class and its Subdivisions, see the Classified Part of the catalogue under the Class Number V44, 31:3 N59

Class Index Entries

INDIA.

For document in this Class and its Subdivisions, see the Classified Part of the catalogue under the Class Number V44, 31:3 N59

Author Index Entry

SHARMA (RK) and others.

Functions of Parliament India.

V44, 31:3 N59

Editor B.I. Entry

GULANI (H) and Others, Ed.
Sharma and Others: Functions of Parliament in India.
V44, 31:3 N59

Series B.I. Entry

POLITICAL SCIENCE SERIES
11 Sharma and others: Functions of Parliament in India.
V44, 31:3 N59

Problem : Authors name merged with title

HEGEL'S LECTURES **ON** **THE HISTORY OF PHILOSOPHY** **Translated from the German** **By** **E.S. Haldane** **Third Edition** **LONDON** **PUTNAM PUBLISHERS** **1959** **(Philosophy Lectures. 7)**

Other informations

Call Number : R855xL7 J5

Acc. No. : 734

First published in England, 1892, Reprinted 1955

Full Name : George Wilhelum Friedrich Hegel, 1770-1831

Main Entry

R855xL7 J5
HEGEL (George Wilhelum Friedrich) (1770-1831).
Lectures on the history of Philosophy. Ed 3. Tr from the German by ES Haldane. (Philosophical lectures. 7).

Tracing

Collection, German Philosophy
German Philosophy.
Philosophy.
Hegel (George Welhelum Friedrich) (1770-1831)
Haldane (ES), Tr.
Lectures on the history of Philosophy.
Philosophical lectures.

Main Entry

COLLECTION, GERMAN PHILOSOPHY
For document in this Class and its Subdivisions, see the Classified Part of the catalogue under the Class Number R855xL7 J5

GERMAN PHILOSOPHY.

For document in this Class and its Subdivisions, see the Classified Part of the catalogue under the Class Number R855

PHILOSOPHY.

For document in this Class and its Subdivisions, see the Classified Part of the catalogue under the Class Number R

HEGEL (George Wilhelum Friedrich) (1770-1831).

Lectures on the history of Philosophy. Ed. 3.

R855xL7 J5

HALDANE (ES), Tr.

Hegel : Lectures on the history of Philosophy.

R855xL7 J5

LECTURES ON the history of Philosophy.
By Hegel. R855xL7 J5

PHILOSOPHICAL LECTURES.
7 Hegel: Lectures on the history of Philosophy. R855xL7 J5

Problem : Pseudonym name of author given on title page

> **PREMCHAND**
>
> **SEVA SADAN**
>
> **7th Reprint**
>
> **Hindi Pracharak Samiti**
> **JHANSI**

Other informations

Call Number : 0-,3 'N

Acc. No. : 3175

0-, 3 'N
PREMCHAND, Pseud
Sevasadan.

FICTION, HINDI, LITERATURE.
For documents in this Class
. . . . Under the Class Number
0-,3'

HINDI, LITERATURE.
For documents in this Class
. . . Under the Class Number
0-,

Problem : Pseudonym name with real name in the book

> **MY EVILS**
>
> **A philosophical study**
>
> **Armstrong**
> **(Ramsey Donald)**
>
> **Translated by**
> **George Allen**
>
> **Third Edition**
>
> **George & Co.**
> **London**
> **1943**

Call Number : R4915 N4

Acc. No. : 2130

Page : X1,218

Size : 23cm.

Literature.
For documents in this Class
. . . Under the Class Number
0

PREM CHAND, Pseud.
Sevasadan. 0-,3 'N
For documents in this Class
. . . Under the Class Number
0

SEVASADAN.
By Premchand, Pseud.
0-,3 'N

R4915 N4
ARMSTRONG, Pseud, (ie Ramsey Donald).
My evils : A Philosophical study.
Ed 3. Tr by George Allen.

2130

Tracing

Evils, Philosophy.

Philosophy.

Armstrong, Pseud. (ie Ramsey Donald).

Allen (George), Tr, My evils : A Philosophical study.

Donald (Ramsey).

EVILS, PHILOSOPHY.		
	For documents in this Class	
. .	. . Under the Class Number	
		R 4915

PHILOSOPHY.		
	For documents in this Class	
. .	. Under the Class Number	
		R
		.

ARMSTRONG, Pseud, (ie Ramsey Donald).		
	My evils : A philosophical study.	
Ed	3.	R4915 N4

ALLEN (George), Tr.
Armstrong, Pseud : My evils.
R4915 N4

MY EVILS.
By Armstrong, Pseud, (ie Ramsey Donald).
Ed.4.
R4915 N4

DONALD (Ramsey).
See
Armstrong, Pseud.

Problem : Real name on title page but Pseudonym name from outside source

> **Outside readings in American Government**
>
> **By**
>
> **Nevil Shute Norway**
>
> **Second Revised Edition**
>
> **New York**
> **MORROW**
> **1949**

Other informations

Call Number : W6.73 K3

Acc. No. : 3621

Page : 318

Size : 22cm.

The author is also known with his Pseudonym name Nevil Shute.

W 6.73 K3
NORWAY (Nevil Shute), (ie Nevil Shute, Pseud).
Outside reading in American Government, Rev. Ed 2.

3621

Tracing

United States, Democracy, Political Science.
Democracy, Political Science.
Political Science.
Norway (Nevil Shute), (ie Nevil Shute, Pseud).
Outside reading in American Government.

Nevil Shute, Pseud.

UNITED STATES, DEMOCRACY, POLITICAL SCIENCE.
For documents in this Class
. . . Under the Class Number
W6.73

DEMOCRACY, POLITICAL SCIENCE.
For documents in this Class
. . . Under the Class Number
R6

POLITICAL SCIENCE.
For documents in this Class
. . . Under the Class Number
R

NORWAY (Nevil Shute), (ie Nevil Shute, Pseud).
Outside readings in American Government.
Rev ed 2.
R6.73 K3

OUTSIDE READINGS in American Government.
By Norway.
R6.73 K3

NEVIL SHUTE , Pseud.

See

NORWAY (Nevil Shute).

Problem : Anonymous book with Calloborator

The Divine LOVE **Translation of the** **Bhagwad Gita** **By R.K. Chakravorty**   **Dass & Co.** **Calcutta** **1941**

Other informations

Call Number : R66,6 N41

Acc. No. : 1234

Page : 7X , 372

Size : 22cm.

R66,6 N41
CHAKRAVORTY (RK), Tr.
Divine LOVE : Translation of
Bhagwad Gita,

1234

Tracing

Bhagwad Gita, Indian Philosophy.
Indian Philosophy.
Philosophy.
Chakravorty (RK), Tr.

Divine LOVE.

BHAGWAD GITA, INDIAN.
PHILOSOPHY,
For document in this Class and its Subdivisions, see the Classified Part of the catalogue under the Class Number

R66,6

INDIAN PHILOSOPHY.
For documents in this Class
. . Under the Class Number
R66,

PHILOSOPHY.
For documents in this Class
. . . Under the Class Number
R

CHAKRAVORTY (RK), Tr.
Divine God.
R 66,6 N41

Other entry will have heading Title — DIVINE LOVE.

Problem : Anonymous work without Calloborator

DICTIONARY OF LIBRARY SCIENCE
Edition Seventh
Jaysuria Publication   **Madras**   **1957**

Other informations

Call Number : 2k

Acc. No. : 345

	2k	
		LIBRARY SCIENCE (Dictionary of —).
	Ed7.	
	345	

Tracing

Dictionary, LIBRARY SCIENCE.

Library Science.

	DICTIONARY, LIBRARY SCIENCE.	
		For documents in this Class
	. .	. Under the Class Number 2k

Other Class Index Entry —

LIBRARY SCIENCE.

For documents..... Under the Class Number 2

Problem : Series without editor

Mekins Science Series. 7

Elementary Arithmetic and Algebra

By
Sriram Srivastava

Third Edition

Mekins & Co.
London
1978

Other informations

Call Number : B113 N10

Acc. No. : 73

B113,N10
SRIVASTAVA (Sriram).
Elementary arthimetic and
algebra. Ed 3.
(Mekins science series. 7).

73

Tracing

Algebric analysis,
Arithmetic.
Arithmetic.
Srivastava (Sriram).

Mekins Science Series.

ALGEBRIC ANALYSIS, ARITHMETIC.
For documents in this Class
. . . Under the Class Number
B113

ARITHMETIC.
For documents in this Class
. . . Under the Class Number B

SRIVASTAVA (Sriram).
Elementary arithmetic and
algebra. Ed.3 B113,N1

MEKINS SCIENCE SERIES
7 Srivastava : Elementary arithmetic
and algebra. B113,N1

Problem : Series with editor.

An Introduction **to the** **Fields of Psychology** **By** **Emily S. Dexter** **K.T. Omwake** **New York** **Prentice Hall Inc.** **1938**

Other informations

Call Number : S N38

Acc. No. : 821

Note : Prentice Hall Psychology Series /
F.A. Mass, Editor / It is 22 in list.

	S	N 38
		DEXTER (Emily S) and OMWAKE (KT).
		Introduction to the field of Psychology.
		(Prentice Hall Psychology series.
	Ed	by F.A.Mass.22).
	821	

Tracing

Psychology.
Dexter (Emily S) AND.
Omwake (KT).
Omwake (KT) and Dexter
(Emily S).
Prentice Hall Psychology
Series.

Mass (FA), Ed.

	PSYCHOLOGY.	
		For documents in this Class
	. .	. Under the Class Number S

DEXTER (Emily S) and OMWAKE (KT).
Introduction to the field of Psychology.
S N38

OMWAKE (KT) and DEXTER (Emily S).
Introduction to the field of psychology.
S N38

PRENTICE HALL PSYCHOLOGY SERIES.
Dexter and Omwake : Introduction To the field of psychology.
S N38

Problem : Independent Series

Engineering in
UNITED STATES
A report

By
F. Faster
G. Schaler

Manchester
University Press
1906

Other informations

Call Number : D6 (X).73

Acc. No. : 94

University of Manchester Publications No. 12

Manchester University Economic Series. 3

Main Entry

D6(X).73; N) N06
FOSTER (Frank) and SCHOLAR
(Girtside).
Engineering in United States:
A Report on Industry and Commerce.
(University of Manchester Publication.
22).
(Manchester University Economic
Series.3).
94

Tracing

United States, Economics,
Electrical Engineering.
Economics, Electrical
Engineering.
Electrical Engineering.
Engineering.
Foster (Frank) and Scholar
(Girtside).
Scholar (Girtside) and Foster
(Frank).
University of Manchester Publication
Manchester University Economics Series

Class Index Entry

UNITED STATES, ECONOMICS,
ELECTRICAL ENGINEERING.
For documents in this Class
. . . Under the Class Number
D6(X).73

Class Index Entry

ECONOMICS, ELECTRICAL ENGINEERING.
For documents in this Class
. . . Under the Class Number
D6(X)

Class Index Entry

ELECTRICAL ENGINEERING.
For documents in this Class
. . . Under the Class Number
D6(X)

Author Index Entry

FOSTER (Frank) and SCHOLAR (Girtside).
Engineering in United States:
D6(X).73 'N1 N06

J+Author Index Entry

SCHOLAR (Girtside) and FOSTER
(Frank).
Engineering in United States.
D6(X).73 'N1 N06

Series Index Entry

UNIVERSITY OF MANCHESTER
PUBLICATIONS.
22 Foster and Scholar : Engineering
in United States.
D6(X).73 'N1 N06

Series Index Entry

MANCHESTER UNIVERSITY ECONOMIC.
SERIES.
3 Foster and Scholar : Engineering
In United States.
D6(X).73 'N1 N06

Problem : Subordinate Series

> **Rajasthan Historical Series**
> **Archeological**
> **studies. 17**
>
> **HISTORICAL MONUMENTS**
>
> **By**
> **V.P. Parmar**
>
> **VKRV Publications**
> **Jaipur**
> **1989**

Other informations

Call Number : V4482:7

Acc. No. : 3123

ISBN 0-3597-321

Note : Dr. S.V. Pandey is editor of the series.

V4482:7 N89
PARMAR (VP).
Historical Monuments.
(Rajasthan Historical series;
Archeological studies. Ed by 5V
Pandey).

3123

Tracing

Archeology. Rajasthan
History.
Rajasthan, History
History.
Parmar (VP).
Rajasthan Historical series,
Archeological studies.

Pandey (SV), Ed.

ARCHEOLOGY. RAJASTHAN.
HISTORY.
For documents in this Class
. . . Under the Class Number
V4482:7

RAJASTHAN. HISTORY.
For documents in this Class
. . . Under the Class Number
V4482

HISTORY.
For documents in this Class
. . . Under the Class Number
V

PARMAR (VP).
Historical monuments

RAJASTHAN HISTORICAL
SERIES. ARCHEOLOGICAL
STUDIES.
17 Parmar : Historical monuments.
V4482:7 N89

PANDEY (SV), Ed.
See
RAJASTHAN HISTORICAL
SERIES.

HISTORICAL MONUMENTS.
By Parmar.
V4482:7 N89

Problem : Pseudo Series

POLITICAL HISTORY OF INDIA

Nikhil Kumar

(Political history of India No. 4 Ed. by Romal L. Singh)

Jogi Publications
Mumbai
1923

Other informations

Call Number : V44 N23

Acc. No. : 5317

Page X1,219

Size 24cm.

V44 N23
NIKHIL KUMAR.
Political history of India
(1315-1417).
Political history of India / Ed
By Romal L Singh.4).

5317

INDIA, HISTORY.
HISTORY.
NIKHIL KUMAR.

Political history of
India.

Singh (Romal L), Ed.

INDIA HISTORY.
For documents in the Class
. . . Under the Class Number
V44 N23

HISTORY.
For documents in this class
.... under the Class Number
V44 N23

NIKHIL KUMAR.
Political history of India
(1315-1417).
(Political history of India.
Ed by Romal L Singh).
V44 N23

5317

POLITICAL HISTORY OF INDIA.
4 Nikhil Kumar: Political history
of India. V44 N23

SINGH (Romal L Singh), Ed.
See
POLITICAL HISTORY OF INDIA.

Problem : Thesis Series

> **UNIVERSITY LIBRARY**
>
> **Its Management and organisation in INDIA**
>
> **By**
>
> **Dr. C.K. Sharma**
>
> **(Ph.D. Thesis awarded by Ravishankar University)**
>
> **in**
>
> **1977**
>
> **Delhi**
>
> **Metropolitan Book Co.**

Other informations

Call Number :	234; 494:8
Acc. No. :	2931
Page	289
Size	23cm.

234;494:8.44 N77
SHARMA (CK).
University Library: Its Management and organisation in India.
(Ravi Shankar University, thesis (Ph.D). 1977).

2931

Tracing

INDIA, ADMINISTRATION, THESIS (Ph.D.).
UNIVERSITY LIBRARY SCIENCE.
MANAGEMENT, THESIS, UNIVERSITY, LIBRARY SCIENCE.
THESIS, UNIVERSITY, LIBRARY SCIENCE.
UNIVERSITY LIBRARY.
LIBRARY SCIENCE.
Sharma (CK)
Ravishankar University, Thesis. (Ph.D.). 1977

INDIA, ADMINISTRATION, THESIS (Ph.D.)
UNIVERSITY, LIBRARY SCIENCE.
For documents in this class
..... under the Class Number
234; 494:8.44

ADMINISTRATION, THESIS (Ph.D.),
UNIVERSITY, LIBRARY SCIENCE.
For documents in this class
..... under the Class Number
234; 494:8

THESIS (Ph.D.), UNIVERSITY LIBRARY
SCIENCE.
For documents in this class
..... under the Class Number
234; 494

UNIVERSITY LIBRARY SCIENCE.
For documents in this class
..... under the Class Number
234

LIBRARY SCIENCE.
For documents in this class
..... under the Class Number
2

SHARMA (CK).
University Library: Its management and organisation in India.
(Ravishankar University, Thesis (Ph.D.) 1977).

RAVISHANKAR UNIVERSITY, Thesis (Ph.D.) 1977 SHARMA: University Library.
234;494:8.44 N77

Problem : Corporate body

INDIA's

Foreign Policy during 70s:
A step for peace and cooperation

Excerpts from the lectures of
President V.V. Giri on Foreign
policy and role of India

Published by:
Publication Division
Government of India
New Delhi
1972

Other informations

Call Number : V44, 1:19y7 K7

Acc. No. : 2341

It is number 12 in India's Foreign Policy Series.

Main Entry

V44, 1:19y7 K7
INDIA, PRESIDENT (V.V. Giri).
India's Foreign Policy during 70:
A step for peace and cooperation.
(India's Foreign Policy Series. 12).

2341

Tracing

Report, Foreign Policy, President, India, History.
Foreign Policy, President, India, History.
President, India, History
India, History
History.
President (VV Giri).
India's Foreign Policy Series.

REPORT, FOREIGN POLICY, PRESIDENT,
INDIA, HISTORY.
For documents in this class
...... under the Class Number
V44, 1:19y7

FOREIGN POLICY, PRESIDENT, INDIA, HISTORY.

For documents in this class

...... under the Class Number

V44, 1: 19

PRESIDENT, INDIA, HISTORY. LIBRARY SCIENCE.

For documents in this class

...... under the Class Number

V44, 1:19

PRESIDENT, INDIA, HISTORY.

For documents in this class

...... under the Class Number

V44, 1

INDIA HISTORY.

For documents in this class

...... under the Class Number

V44

HISTORY.
For documents in this class
...... under the Class Number
V

INDIA PRESIDENT (VV Giri).
India's foreign policy in
70's : A step for peace and cooperation.
(India's foreign policy series. 12).
V44, 1:19y7 K7

2341

INDIA'S FOREIGN POLICY SERIES.
12 India. President (VV Giri): India's
Foreign policy:
V44, 1:19y7 k7

Problem : Corporate body

RURAL HIGHER EDUCATION MANUAL Ministry of Education Government of India Illustrated New Delhi Manager of Publications 1969

Other informations

Call Number : T4-9 (Y31)y8

Acc. No. : 2101

Main Entry

T4-9 (Y31)y8 N59

INDIA, EDUCATION (Ministry of —).

Rural higher education manual.

2101

Tracing

Manual Rural Community,
Higher Education.
Rural Community, Higher Education,
Higher Education.
Education.
INDIA, EDUCATION (Ministry of —).

MANUAL, RURAL COMMUNITY, HIGHER EDUCATION.

For documents in this class

...... under the Class Number

T4-9 (Y31)y8

RURAL COMMUNITY, HIGHER EDUCATION.

For documents in this class

...... under the Class Number

T4-9 (Y31)

HIGHER EDUCATION.

For documents in this class

...... Under the Class Number

T4

EDUCATION.

For documents in this class

...... under the Class Number

T

INDIA, EDUCATION (Ministry of —).

Rural higher education manual.

T4-9 (Y31) y8 N59

Problem : Single Corporate body

Government of Madras
LEGISLATIVE DEPARTMENT
INDIAN COUNCILS ACTS 1861 to 1909 (Rules and Regulations)
Madras Superintendent, Government Press 1910

Other informations

Call Number : V442, 3; (zq)'N1 N10

Acc. No. : 321

Pages 278

Size 23cm.

V442,3; (zq)'N1 N10

MADRAS, LEGISLATIVE (Department).

Indian Councils Acts, 1861-1909: Rules and regulations.

321

Tracing

Rules and regulations, Legislature, Madras, History.
Legislature, Madras, History.
Madras History.
History.
Madras, Legislative (Department).
Indian Councils Act, 1861-1909: Rules and regulations.

RULES AND REGULATIONS, LEGISLATURE,

For document in this Class and its Subdivisions, see the Classified Part of the catalogue under the Class Number V442,3; (zq)

LEGISLATURE, MADRAS, HISTORY.

For document in this Class and its Subdivisions, see the Classified Part of the catalogue under the Class Number V442,3

MADRAS, HISTORY.

For documents in this Class

...... under the Class Number

V442

HISTORY

For documents in this Class

...... under the Class Number

V

MADRAS, LEGISLATIVE (Department).
Indian Councils Acts, 1861-1909:
Rules and regulations.
V442, 3; (zq)'N1 N10

INDIAN COUNCILS Act, 1861-1909:
Rules and Regulations.
By Madras, Legislature (Department).
V442, 3; (zq)'N1 N10

Problem : Two Corporate bodies

DIABETES FACT BOOK **U.S. Department** **Department of Health, Education and Welfare** **Public Health Centre** **Division of Chronic Diseases** **Washington, D.C.** **Government Printing Office** **Washington** **1961**

Other informations

Call Number : L293:46.73K1

Acc. No. : 2310

Public Health Service Publication No. 890.

Page 279

Size 22cm.

L293: 46.73 K61

UNITED STATES, HEALTH, EDUCATION and WELFARE (Department), PUBLIC HEALTH (Centre), CHRONIC DISEASE (Division of —).

Diabetes fact book.

(Public Health Service Publication. 890).

279

Tracing

UNITED STATES, DISEASE, DIABETES, MEDICINE.
DISEASE, DIABETES, MEDICINE
DIABETES, MEDICINE.
MEDICINE.
United States, Health, Education and Welfare (Department), Public (Division of —)
Health Education and Welfare (Department), Public Health (Centre), Chronic disease (Division of —).
Public health service publication.

UNITED STATES, DISEASE, DIABETES, MEDICINE.

For documents in this Class ..... under the Class Number

V293:46.73 K61

DISEASE, DIABETES, MEDICINE.
For documents in this Class
...... under the Class Number
L293:46

DIABETES, MEDICINE.
For documents in this Class
...... under the Class Number
L293

MEDICINE
For documents in this Class
...... under the Class Number
L

UNITED STATES, HEALTH, EDUCATION
and WELFARE (Department), PUBLIC
HEALTH (Centre), CHRONIC DISEASE
(Division of —).
Diabetes fact book.
L293:46.73 K61

PUBLIC HEALTH SERVICE PUBLICATION.
890 Health, education and welfare (Department),
...... etc : Diabetes fact book.
L293: 46.73 K61

Problem : Commissions/Committees

ART AND GOVERNMENT

Report on

Activities of Federal Government in the field of Art

Commission of Fine Art

Washington, D.C.
Govt. of United States Publication Unit
1953

Other informations

Call Number : V73:3 (N)'N51t N53

Acc. No. : 7131

Page 311

Size 23cm.

Note : The Chairman of the Commission was David E Finley.

V73:3 (N)'N51t N53

UNITED STATES, FINE ARTS (Commission of —) (1951) (Chairman : David E Finley).

Art and Government : Report on activities of Federal government in the field of arts.

71131

Tracing

Commission Report, Fine Art, Function, United States, History.
Fine Art, Functions, United States, History.
United States, History.
History.
United States, Fine Arts (Commission of —) (1951) (Chairman : David E Finley).
Fine Art (Commission of —) (1951) (Chairman: David E Finley).

COMMISSION REPORT, FINE ART, FUNCTIONS, UNITED STATES, HISTORY.

For documents in this Class
..... under the Class Number
V73:3 (N)'N51 t

FINE ART, FUNCTIONS, UNITED STATES, HISTORY.
For documents in this Class
...... under the Class Number
L73:3 (N)

FUNCTIONS, UNITED STATES, HISTORY.
For documents in this Class
...... under the Class Number
V73:3

UNITED STATES, HISTORY.
For documents in this Class
...... under the Class Number
V73

HISTORY.
For documents in this Class
...... under the Class Number
V

UNITED STATES, FINE ART, (Commission of —)
(1951) (Chairman : David E Finley).
Art and Government : Report on activities
of Federal government in the field of
arts. V73:3 (N)'N51t N53

FINE ART (Commission of —) (1951)
(Chairman : David E Finley), UNITED
STATES.
Art and Government : Report on
activities of Federal Government in the
field of arts. V73:3 (N)'N51t N53

One more entry

FINLEY (David E), Chairman.

See

UNITED STATES, FINE ART (Commission of —)
(1951).

Problem : Institution as author

American Library Association Committee on Libraries, Committee on Education **PRISON LIBRARY HANDBOOK** American Prison Association Editor-in-Chief. E.K. Jones Chicago American Library Association 1932

Other informations

Call Number :	2, 62	N32
Acc. No. :	2132	
Page	257	
Size	22cm.	

2.63 N 32

LIBRARY (American-Association), LIBRARY (Commission-in correctional Institutions), PRISON (American-Association), EDUCATION (Committee on —).

Prison library handbook. Ed by EK Jones.

2132

Tracing

Prison Library, Library Science.
Library Science.
Library (American-Association), Library (Committee on — in Correctional Institutions), Prison (American-Association), Education (Committee on —).
Prison (American-Association), Education (committee on —)
Jones (EK), Ed.

PRISON LIBRARY, LIBRARY SCIENCE.

For documents in this Class ...... under the Class Number 263

LIBRARY SCIENCE.
For documents in this Class
.... under the Class Number 2

LIBRARY (American-Association), LIBRARIES (Committee on—in correctional Institutions),PRISON (American-Association), EDUCATION (Committee on —).
Prison Library handbook.
263 N32

PRISON (American-Association), EDUCATION (Committee on —).
Library (American-Association): Prison Library handbook. 263 N32

JONES (EK), Ed.
LIBRARY (American-Association) :
Prison library handbook.
263 N32

PUBLIC HEALTH SERVICE PUBLICATION.
890 Health, education and welfare (Department),
...... etc: Diabetes fact book.
L293: 46.73 K61

Problem : Institution

Statement on the recommendations of the Indian Statutory Commission

By
Landholders of India

Calcutta
British Indian Association
1932

Other informations

Call Number : V44, 187 'N28't:g (Z44, 211) N32
Acc. No. : 1731
Page 270
Size 23cm.

V44,187 'N28t:g (Z44, 211) N32
LANDHOLDERS (of India) (Calcutta).
Statement on the recommendations of the
Indian Statutory Commission.

1781

Tracing

Land, Law, Commission,
Statutory, India, History.
Law, Commission, Statutory,
India, History.
Commission, Statutory,
India, History.
Statutory, India, History.
India, History.
History.
Landholders (of India)(Calcutta) (1928)
Statement on the recommendations
of the Indian Statutory Commission.

LAND, LAW, COMMISSION, STATUTORY,
INDIA, HISTORY.
For documents in this Class
..... under the Class Number
V44, 187 'N28t:g (Z44, 211)

LAW, COMMISSION, STATUTORY, INDIA, HISTORY.

For documents in this Class

..... under the Class Number

V44, 187 'N28t:g (Z)

COMMISSION, STATUTORY, INDIA, HISTORY.

For documents in this Class

..... under the Class Number

V44, 187 'N28t

STATUTORY, INDIA, HISTORY.

For documents in this Class

..... under the Class Number

V44,187

INDIA, HISTORY.

For documents in this Class

..... under the Class Number

V44

INDIA

For documents in this Class

..... under the Class Number V

STATEMENT ON the recommendations of the Indian Statutory Commission.

By Landholders (— of India) (Calcutta) (1928).

LANDHOLDERS (— of India) (Calcutta) (1928).

Statement on the recommendations of the Indian Statutory Commission.

V44, 187 'N28t:g (Z44, 211)

Problem : Single Institution with series

International Trade Series, 211

TRADE RELATIONS BETWEEN FREE MARKET & CONTROLLED ECONOMICS

Economic, Financial and Transit
Department
League of Nations

Geneva
League of Nations
1943

Other informations

Call Number : X:57-75.1 'N4 H3
Acc. No. : 2134
Pages 217
Size 23cm.

X:57-1 'N4 H3

LEAGUE OF NATIONS (Geneva)
ECONOMIC, FINANCIAL AND TRANSIT
(Department).

Trade relations between free market
and controlled economics.

(International Trade Series. 211).

2134

Tracing

World, Planned Economy,
Foreign exchange, Economics.
Planned economy, Foreign
Exchange, Economics.
Foreign exchange, Economics.
Economics.
League of Nations (Geneva),
Economic, Financial and
Transit (Department).
Trade relations between free
market and controlled economics.
International Trade series.

WORLD, PLANNED ECONOMY, FOREIGN
EXCHANGE, ECONOMICS.

For documents in this Class and its Subdivisions, see the Classified Part of the catalogue under the Class Number X:57-75.1

PLANNED ECONOMY, FOREIGN EXCHANGE, ECONOMICS.

For documents in this Class and its Subdivisions, see the Classified Part of the catalogue under the Class Number X:57-75

FOREIGN EXCHANGE, ECONOMICS.

For documents in this Class and its Subdivisions, see the Classified Part of the catalogue under the Class Number X:57

ECONOMICS.

For documents in this Class and its Subdivisions, see the Classified Part of the catalogue under the Class Number X

LEAGUE OF NATIONS (Geneva), ECONOMIC,
FINANCIAL AND TRANSIT (Department).
Trade relations between free market and
Controlled economics.
X:57-75.1 'N4 H3

INTERNATIONAL TRADE SERIES.
211 League of Nations (Geneva): Trade relations...
Controlled economics.
X:57-75.1 'N4 H3

Problem : Institutions with editors and edition statement

> **SAMPLING INSPECTION**
>
> **Principle procedures and tables for single, double and sequential sampling.**
>
> **By**
> **Statistical Research Group**
> **COLUMBIA UNIVERSITY**
>
> **Edited by:**
> **H.A. Freeman**
> **W.A. Wallis**
>
> **Second Revised Edition**
>
> **New York**
> **McGRAW-HILL BOOK Co.**
> **1948**

Other informations

Call Number :	B:312p2817 N48
Acc. No. :	2130
Pages	317
Size	22cm.

B2817 N48

UNIVERSITY (Columbia), STATISTICAL (Research Group).

Sampling inspection : Principles, procedures and tables for single and double and sequential sampling. Rev ed 2. Ed by HA Freeman and W A Wallis.

2130

Tracing

Sampling Statistics, Mathematics.
Mathematics.
University (Columbia), Statistical
(Research Group).
Freeman (HA) and Wallis
(WA), Ed.
Wallis (WA) and Freeman (HA),
Ed.

SAMPLING STATISTICS, MATHEMATICS.

For documents in this Class and its Subdivisions, see the Classified Part of the catalogue under the Class Number B2817

MATHEMATICS.

For documents in this Class and its Subdivisions, see the Classified Part of the catalogue under the Class Number B

UNIVERSITY (Columbia), STATISTICAL (Research Group).

Sampling inspection : Principles, procedures and tables for single and double..... sampling. Rev ed 2. Ed by HA Freeman and WA Wallis.

B2817 N48

FREEMAN (HA) and WALLIS (WA), Ed.

University (Columbia), Statistical (Research Group): Sampling inspection:

B2817 N48

WALLIS (WA) and FREEMAN (HA), Ed.

University (Columbia), Statistical (Research Group): Sampling inspection:

B2817 N48

Problem : Conference

ALL INDIA
CONFERENCE OF LIBRARIANS

Held at Lahore
Jan 4-8, 1918

Proceedings

Simla
Government Press
1918

Other informations

Call Number : 2p44, N18 N18
Acc. No. : 210
Pages 318
Size 23cm.

2p44, N18 N18

ALL INDIA CONFERENCE OF LIBRARIANS. (Lahore) (1918).

Proceedings.

210

Tracing

India, Conference proceedings, Library Science.

Conference proceedings, Library Science.

All India Conference of Librarians (Lahore) (1918).

INDIA, CONFERENCE PROCEEDINGS, LIBRARY SCIENCE.

For documents in this Class and its Subdivisions, see the Classified Part of the catalogue under the Class Number 2p44

CONFERENCE PROCEEDINGS, LIBRARY SCIENCE.
For documents in this Class and its Subdivisions, see the Classified Part of the catalogue under the Class Number 2p

LIBRARY SCIENCE.
For documents in this Class and its Subdivisions, see the Classified Part of the catalogue under the Class Number 2

ALL INDIA CONFERENCE OF LIBRARIANS (Lahore) (1918).
Proceedings. 2p44,N18 N18

Problem : Seminar with sponsoring body

NATIONAL SEMINAR
on
PLANT BREEDING
(New Delhi. Jan 1957)

PROCEEDINGS

Indian Society of Genetics

Asia Science Office
New Delhi
1967

Other informations

Call Number : J:6p1, N57 J6
Acc. No. : 2317
Pages 213
Size 22cm.

J:6p44, N57 N6

GENETICS (Indian Society of—), National Seminar on Plant breeding (New Delhi) (1957).

Proceedings.

2317

Tracing

India, Conference proceedings, Genetics, Agriculture.
Conference proceedings, Genetics, Agriculture.
Genetics, Agriculture.
Agriculture.
Genetics (Indian Society of—), National Seminar on plant breeding (New Delhi) (1957).
National Seminar on plant breeding, Genetics (Indian society of—) (New Delhi) (1957).
Proceedings.

INDIA, CONFERENCE PROCEEDINGS,
GENETICS, AGRICULTURE.

For documents in this Class and its Subdivisions, see the Classified Part of the catalogue under the Class Number J:6p44

CONFERENCE PROCEEDINGS, GENETICS, AGRICULTURE.

For documents in this Class and its Subdivisions, see the Classified Part of the catalogue under the Class Number J:6p

GENETICS, AGRICULTURE.

For documents in this Class and its Subdivisions, see the Classified Part of the catalogue under the Class Number J:6

AGRICULTURE.

For documents in this Class and its Subdivisions, see the Classified Part of the catalogue under the Class Number J

GENETICS (Indian Society of —) NATIONAL SEMINAR ON PLANT BREEDING (New Delhi) (1957).

Proceedings.

J:6p44, N57 N6

NATIONAL SEMINAR ON PLANT BREEDING
GENETICS (Indian Society of —) (New Delhi)
(1957).
Proceedings.
J:6p44, N57 N6

PROCEEDINGS.
By Genetics (Indian Society of —) (New Delhi)
(1957), National Seminar on Plant breeding.
J:6p44, N57 N6

Problem : Pseudonymous author with real name given

> **HISTORY OF INDIA**
>
> **By**
> **An Indian**
>
> **1962**
> **Meakins Publications**
> **Calcutta**

Other informations

Call Number : V44 'N6 N62

Acc. No. : 2131

Pages 173

Size 22cm.

Note : Authors real name is Ramanna.

V44 'N6 N62

INDIAN, Pseud, (*i.e.* Ramanna)

History of India.

2131

Tracing

India, History,
History.

Ramanna.

INDIA, HISTORY

For documents in this Class and its Subdivisions, see the Classified Part of the catalogue under the Class Number V44

HISTORY.

For documents in this Class and its Subdivisions, see the Classified Part of the catalogue under the Class Number V

INDIAN, Pseud. (*i.e.* Ramanna).

History of India.

V44, N6 N62

RAMANNA.

See

INDIAN, Pseud.

Problem : Independent series with Pseudonym author

THE WORLD OF PREMCHAND (Selected stories of Premchand) Translated by David Rubin George Allen and Unwin Ltd. London 1895

Other informations

Call Number : 0152, 3M80x111 K9

Acc. No. : 1032

Pages 312

Size 22cm.

Note : Unesco collection of Representative Works, 31, Asian Fiction Series 3.

0152, 3M80x 111 K9

PREMCHAND, Pseud, (*i.e.* Dhanpat Rai).

World of Premchand : Selected stories of Premchand. Tr by David Rubin.

(Unesco collection of representative works. 31; Asian Fiction Series. 3).

1032

Tracing

Works, Premchand, Pseud.
Fiction, Hindi.
Hindi Literature.
Literature.
Rubin (David), Tr.
Unesco collection of representative works
Asian fiction series.

Rai (Dhanpat)

WORKS, PREMCHAND, Pseud.

For documents in this Class and its Subdivisions, see the Classified Part of the catalogue under the Class Number 0152,3M80x 111

FICTION, HINDI.

For documents in this Class and its Subdivisions, see the Classified Part of the catalogue under the Class Number 0152,3

HINDI LITERATURE.

For documents in this Class and its Subdivisions, see the Classified Part of the catalogue under the Class Number 0152

LITERATURE.

For documents in this Class and its Subdivisions, see the Classified Part of the catalogue under the Class Number 0

RUBIN (David), Tr.

Premchand, Pseud: World of Premchand: Selected stories of Premchand.

0152,3 M80x 111 K9

UNESCO COLLECTION OF REPRESENTATIVE WORKS.

31 Premchand, Pseud : World of Premchand.

V152, 3M80x 111K9

ASIAN FICTION SERIES.

3 Premchand, Pseud : World of Premchand

V152,3M80x 111K9

RAI (Dhanpat).

See

PREMCHAND, Pseud.

Problem : Multifocal book with personal author and series

> **Columbia Biological Series.11.**
> **Gen. Editor. L.C. Dunn.**
>
> **GENETICS**
> **AND**
> **THE ORIGIN OF SPECIES**
>
> **By**
> **T. Dobzhauskey**
> **Professor of Zoology**
> **Columbia University**
>
> **3rd Edition-Revised**
>
> **COLUMBIA UNIVERSITY PRESS**
> **NEW YORK**
> **1851**

Other informations

Call Number : G:66 N51

Acc. No. : 1721

Pages 378

Size 23cm.

Note : Bibliography appears on page 371-378.

G : 66 N51
DOBZHAUSKEY (T).
Genetics and the origin of species.
Rev ed 3.
(Columbia Biological series. Ed by
LC Dunn. 11).

1721

Tracing

Evaluation; Biology.
Genetics, Biology.
Biology.
Dobzhauskey (T).
Columbia Biological series.
Dunn (LC)

EVOLUTION. BIOLOGY.
For documents in this Class and its Subdivisions, see the Classified Part of the catalogue under the Class Number G:66

FICTION, HINDI.

For documents in this Class and its Subdivisions, see the Classified Part of the catalogue under the Class Number 0152,3

GENETICS. BIOLOGY.

For documents in this Class and its Subdivisions, See the Classified Part of the catalogue under the Class Number G:6

BIOLOGY.

For documents in this Class and its Subdivisions, see the Classified Part of the catalogue under the Class Number G

DOBZHAUSKEY (T).

Genetics and the origin of species.

Rev ed 3. G:66 N51

COLUMBIA BIOLOGICAL SERIES.
11 Dobzhauskey : Genetics and the
origin of species.
G:66 N51

DUNN (LC).
See
COLUMBIA BIOLOGICAL SERIES.

Problem : Multi-Volume Book

> **SRI**
> **GURU-GRANTHA SAHIB**
> **(English Version)**
>
> **Volume 1**
> **(in Four Volumes)**
>
> **Translated by**
> **Dr. Gopal Singh**
>
> **Delhi**
> **Gurudwara Prabandh Samiti**
> **1960**

Other informations

Call Number : Q8441:2 KO

Acc. No. : 230

Note : 1. The work is in 4 volumes. Only volumes 1, 2 are available in library.

2. This scripture is also known as 'Adi Granth' and 'Granth Sahib'.

Q8441:2 KO

GURU GRANTH SAHIB (English Version). Tr by Gopal Singh. 4V. [V3-4 not in library].

230

Tracing

Sacred book, Sikhism, Religion.
Sikhism, Religion.
Religion.
Guru Granth Sahib.
Gopal Singh, Tr.

Adi Granth.
Granth Sahib

SACRED BOOK, SIKHISM, RELIGION.

For documents in this Class and its Subdivisions, see the Classified Part of the catalogue under the Class Number Q8441:2

SIKHISM, RELIGION.
For documents in this Class and its Subdivisions, see the Classified Part of the catalogue under the Class Number Q8441

RELIGION.
For documents in this Class and its Subdivisions, see the Classified Part of the catalogue under the Class Number Q

GURU GRANTH SAHIB (English Version).
Tr by Gopal Singh. 4V. [V3-4 not in library].
Q8441 : 2 KO

SINGH (Gopal), Tr.
Guru Granth Sahib (English Version).
4V. [V3-4 not in library].
Q8441:2 KO

ADI-GRANTH.

See

GURU GRANTH SAHIB.

GRANTH SAHIB.

See

GURU GRANTH SAHIB.

Problem : Multi-Volume book

Commonwealth Studies. 71
HUMAN PROBLEMS OF INDUSTRIAL COMMUNITIES WITHIN THE COMMONWEALTH EMPIRE
By
George Allen
Vol. 1
Reports and Papers
London
Oxford University Press
1956

Other informations

Call Number : X:97. 3, N56J6.1-J6.2

Acc. No. : 3213-4

Volume 2 : Background papers and index.

X:97.3, N56 J6.1 – J6.2
ALLEN (George).
Human problems of industrial communities within the commonwealth empire. 2V.
(Commonwealth studies. 71).
V1. Report and proceedings.
V2. Background papers and index.

3213-4

Tracing

Commonwealth, Industrial relations, Economics.
Industrial relations, Economics.
Economics.
Allen (George).
Human problems of industrial communities within the commonwealth empire.
Commonwealth studies.

COMMONWEALTH, INDUSTRIAL RELATIONS, ECONOMICS.
For documents in this Class and its Subdivisions, see the Classified Part of the catalogue, under the Class Number X : 97.3

INDUSTRIAL RELATIONS, ECONOMICS.

For documents in this Class and its Subdivisions, see the Classified Part of the catalogue under the Class Number X:97

ECONOMICS.

For documents in this Class and its Subdivisions, see the Classified Part of the catalogue under the Class Number X

ALLEN (George).

Human problems of industrial communities within the commonwealth empire. 2V.

(Commonwealth studies. 71).

X:97.3, N56 J6.1-J6.2

HUMAN PROBLEMS of industrial
communities within the Commonwealth Empire.
By Allen. 2V.
X:97.3, N56 J6.1-J6.2

COMMONWEALTH STUDIES.
71 Allen : Human problems of industrial
...... Empire. 2V.
X:97.3, N56 J6.1-J6.2

Problem : Periodical (Simple)

<table border="1"><tr><td>

HERALD OF LIBRARY SCIENCE

Volume No. 1 Jan. 1962

Sponsored by Sarla Ranganathan Endowment for Library Science

</td></tr></table>

Other informations

Call Number : 2m44, N62

Library have all volumes till date.

2m44, N62

HERALD OF library science, (Sarla Ranganathan Endowment for library science).

[IV per year. VI – ; 1962 –].

This library has VI-42; 1962-2003.

Tracing

VI-42 1962-2003 N62-P83 215-56 Library Science.
Periodical, Library Science.
India, Periodical, Library Science.
Periodical.
Periodical.
Sarda Ranganathan Endowment for library science, Herald of Library science.
Herald of library science, Sarda Ranganathan Endowment for library science.

Class Index Entries (Ordinary)

LIBRARY SCIENCE.

For documents in this Class and its Subdivisions, see the Classified Part of the catalogue under the Class Number 2

PERIODICAL, LIBRARY SCIENCE.

For documents in this Class and its Subdivisions, see the Classified Part of the catalogue under the Class Number 2m

INDIA, PERIODICAL, LIBRARY SCIENCE.

For documents in this Class and its Subdivisions, see the Classified Part of the catalogue under the Class Number 2m44

Class Index Entries (Specific)

HERALD OF library science, (Sarda Ranganathan Endowment for library science).

2m44, N62

SARDA RANGANATHAN ENDOWMENT
FOR LIBRARY SCIENCE, Herald of library
science.
2m44, N62

Class Index Entry (Generic)

PERIODICAL.
Herald of library science, (Sarda Ranganathan
Endowment for library science).
2m44, N62

PERIODICAL.
Sarda Ranganathan Endowment
for library science, Herald of library science.
2m44, N62

Problem : Broken issues in library

JOURNAL OF CHEMICAL SOCIETY OF INDIA

Volume 21
No. 1
Jan. 1975

Published by
Chemical Society of India

Other informations

Class Number : Em44, N75

Acc. No. : 623

Note : The library has all volumes till date except Vol. No. 3-4 and 9-11.

Em44, N75
JOURNAL, Chemical Society of India.
[IV per year. VI – ; 1975 –]
This library has VI – 2; 1975 – 76. V5-8; 1978-81. V12 – 29; 1985 – 2003.

Tracing

1-2 1975-76 N75-N76 715-6
5-8 1978-81 N78-N81 717-20
12-29 1985-2003 N85-P81 721-38

Chemistry.
Periodical, Chemistry.
India, Periodical, Chemistry.
Periodical.
Periodical.
Chemical Society of India, Journal.
Journal, Chemical Society of India.

Class Index Entry (Ordinary)

CHEMISTRY.
For documents in this Class and its Subdivisions, see the Classified Part of the catalogue under the Class Number E

PERIODICAL, CHEMISTRY.

For documents in this Class and its Subdivisions, see the Classified Part of the catalogue under the Class Number Em

INDIA, PERIODICAL, CHEMISTRY.

For documents in this Class and its Subdivisions, see the Classified Part of the catalogue under the Class Number Em 44

Class Index Entry (Generic)

PERIODICAL.

Journal, Chemical Society of India.

Em44, N75

PERIODICAL.
Chemical Society of India, Journal.
Em44, N75

Class Index Entry (Specific)

JOURNAL, Chemical Society of India.
Em44, N75

CHEMICAL SOCIETY OF INDIA,
Journal. Em44, N75

Problem : Initionym of sponsoring body appearing with Title

AAUP BULLETIN
V26 (4)   **Dec. 1988**
A Publication of the American Association of University Professors

Other informations

Class Number : T4m 73, N45

Note : It is a quarterly magazine. Library has got the complete set except 9-15.

Main Entry

T4m 73, N45

AAUP Bulletin, (American Association of University Professors).

[IV per year. VI – ; 1945 –].

This library has V1-45; 1945-1988.

230

Tracing

V1-44 1945-88 N45-N-88
4978-5021

Education.
University Education.
Periodical, University Education.
United States, Periodical, University Education.
Periodical.
Periodical.
AAUP Bulletin.
American Association of University Professors, Bulletin.
Bulletin, American Association of University Professors.

Class Index Entry (Specific)

AAUP BULLETIN, (American Association of University Professors).

Tm73, N45

AMERICAN ASSOCIATION OF UNIVERSITY PROFESSORS, Bulletin.

T4m73, N45

Class Index Entry (Generic)

PERIODICAL.

AAUP Bulletin, (American Association of University Professors).

T4m73, N45

PERIODICAL.

American Association of University Professors, Bulletin.

74m73, N45

SINGH (Gopal), Tr.

Guru Granth Sahib (English Version). 4V. [V3-4 not in library].

Q8441:2 KO

Class Index Entry (Ordinary)

UNIVERSITY EDUCATION.

For documents in this Class and its Subdivisions, see the Classified Part of the catalogue under the Class Number T4

EDUCATION.

For documents in this Class and its Subdivisions, see the Classified Part of the catalogue under the Class Number T

UNITED STATES, PERIODICAL, UNIVERSITY EDUCATION.

For documents in this Class and its Subdivisions, see the Classified Part of the catalogue under the Class Number T4m73

Problem : Change of Title

LIBRARY SCIENCE WITH A SLANT TO DOCUMENTATION AND INFORMATION STUDIES
Published and sponsored by SARDA RANGANATHAN ENDOWMENT FOR LIBRARY SCIENCE Bangalore

Other informations

Class Number : 2:97m44, N64

Acc. No. : 27cm

Note : The journal was previously published under the title 'Library Science with a slant to documentation' (from VI to 24, 1964 to 1987).

It is a quarterly journal.

Library has all volumes.

Main Entry

2:97m44, N64

LIBRARY SCIENCE with a slant to documentation and information studies, (Sarda Ranganathan Endowment for Library Science).

[IV per year. V25 – ; 1988 –]

This library has V25-40; 1988-2003.

Tracing

India, Periodical, Documentation, Library Science.
Periodical, Documentation, Library Science.
Documentation, Library Science.
Library Science.
Periodical.
Periodical.
Library Science with a slant to Documentation and Information Studies, (Sarda Ranganathan Endowment for Library Science).

Continued on next card

2:97m44,N64

Sarda Ranganathan Endowment for Library Science, Library Science with a slant to documentation and Information studies.

Class Index Entry (Ordinary)

INDIA, PERIODICAL, DOCUMENTATION, LIBRARY SCIENCE.

For documents in this Class and its Subdivisions, see the Classified Part of the catalogue under the Class Number 2:97m44

PERIODICAL, DOCUMENTATION, LIBRARY SCIENCE.

For documents in this Class and its Subdivisions, see the Classified Part of the catalogue under the Class Number 2:97m

DOCUMENTATION, LIBRARY SCIENCE.

For documents in this Class and its Subdivisions, see the Classified Part of the catalogue under the Class Number 2:97

LIBRARY SCIENCE.

For documents in this Class and its Subdivisions, see the Classified Part of the catalogue under the Class Number 2

Class Index Entry (Generic)

PERIODICAL.
Library Science with a slant to Documentation and Information studies, (Sarda Ranganathan Endowment for Library Science).
2:97m44, N64

PERIODICAL
Sarda Ranganathan Endowment for Library Science, Library Science with a slant to documentation and Information studies.
2:97m44, N64

Class Index Entry (Specific)

LIBRARY SCIENCE with a slant to documentation and Information studies, (Sarda Ranganathan Endowment for Library Science).
2:97m44,N64

SARDA RANGANATHAN ENDOWMENT FOR LIBRARY SCIENCE, Library Science with a slant to documentation and Information studies.
2:97m44, N64

Problem : Periodical. Change of Title

QUARTERLY JOURNAL OF MECHANICS AND ENGINEERING **Sponsored by** **British Association of Engineers**

Other informations

Class Number : B7m56, N59

Notes : 1. The title was changed in 1969 as 'Quarterly Journal of Engineers'. Volume Numbers continued without any change with Volume Number 11.

2. Library subscribed the periodical till this year, and continuous.

Main Entry

B7m56, N59

QUARTERLY JOURNAL of Mechanics and Engineering, (British Association of Engineers).

[IV per year. V1-10 ; 1959-68].

This library has V1-10; 1959-68.

Continued on next card

Continued 1

B7m56, N59

QUARTERLY JOURNAL of Engineers, (British Association of Engineers).

[IV per year. V11 – ; 1969 –].

This library has V11-35; 1969-2003.

Tracing 1

Mathematics.
Mathematics, Mechanics.
Periodical, Mechanic, Mathematics.
Mechanic, Mathematics, Periodical.
Periodical.
Periodical.
Quarterly Journal of Mechanics and Engineering, (British Association of Engineers).
British Association of Engineers, Quarterly Journal of Mechanics and Engineer.

Continued on next card

Continued...2

B7m56, N59

Quarterly Journal of Engineers,
(British Association of Engineers).
British Association of Engineers,
Quarterly Journal of Engineers.